The Principles of Classical Dance

The Principles
of Classical
Dance

JOAN LAWSON

with photographs of
Anthony Dowell
by Anthony Crickmay

Alfred·A·Knopf   New York   1980

THIS IS A BORZOI BOOK
PUBLISHED BY ALFRED A. KNOPF, INC.

Library of Congress Cataloging in Publication Data

Lawson, Joan.
The principles of classical dance.

Includes index.
1. Ballet dancing.   I. Title.
GV1788.L356   1980   792.8′2   80-11607
ISBN 0-394-51061-5

Manufactured in the United States of America
First American Edition

A Note on the Type

The text of this book was set in Ehrhardt, a typeface first
released by The Monotype Corporation Limited of London
in 1937. The design of the face was based on a
seventeenth-century type, probably cut by Nicholas Kis,
used at the Ehrhardt foundry in Leipzig. The original cutting
was one of the first typefaces bearing the characteristics
now referred to as "modern."

Printed by Halliday Lithographers, West Hanover,
Massachusetts, from text film prepared in England and
illustration film prepared by Alithochrome Corporation,
Hauppauge, New York, and bound by American Book-
Stratford Press, Saddle Brook, New Jersey.
Format designed by Albert Chiang.

Contents

Illustrations

Each photograph of Anthony Dowell illustrates some of if not all the seven
principles of classical dance; therefore the brief captions are only intended
to name the movement being danced.

Introduction

This book is an attempt to state the principles upon which classical dance and its rules are based. Every art has principles which generate the rules that govern the exercise of creative talent. In some cases rules become so rigid and limiting that artists have seen fit to break them. This has sometimes led to excitingly original forms of art, but at other times to a state of virtual anarchy or a type of art understood only by the followers of a particular artist or cult.

No matter how far dancers and choreographers dismiss or break the rules laid down by such great dancing-masters as Blasis, Bournonville, Cecchetti and Vaganova, the purely classical ballet and its derivatives, the romantic and *demi-caractère* works, still hold their place in the repertoire of companies all over the world. Although Petipa's *Sleeping Beauty*, Fokine's *Firebird* and Ashton's *Fille mal gardée* may all seem very different to newcomers to ballet, they are all based on the same principles of movement—despite the fact that many of the technical rules are broken in order to create a particular style of dance suitable to the subject and its characters.

Principles and rules should all be studied by aspiring dancers and choreographers if they are to create the style and qualities of movement necessary to communicate the mood, emotion, theme and story of any ballet using the medium of classical dance.

This book is also a tribute to Dame Ninette de Valois, whose leadership has marvellously brought the Royal Ballet to pre-eminence. Her wise words form a large part of the text, just as they have become part of the inheritance she has created for her staff at the Royal Ballet School. If her statements are not always given as quotations, it is because for those of us who have had the privilege to work for her they have become so much a part of our own teaching that what we tell our students is spoken in Dame Ninette's own words almost without our realising it.

The English school of classical dance has only gradually taken shape since Dame Ninette began teaching in 1926. Its development was strengthened as Sir Frederick Ashton sought to express not only the moods, emotions and actions of her dancers, but also to express the form and quality of the music he chose to interpret.

From the study of past dancing-masters Dame Ninette created an English style, drawing from the disciplines of the French, Russian and Italian schools to make something of her own. That 'something' is difficult to define. Its particular features are not always appreciated by those who look only at the virtuosity of the soloist and not at the part he or she plays in the whole. Nor is it always appreciated that to play the part of the Prince (*danseur noble*) or Princess (ballerina) is not the same thing as to dance it brilliantly, even though this may be desirable. Dancers who undertake such roles in classical ballet have to play the part as to the manner born and behave as if always in command not only of the court, the stage and every situation that arises, but also of themselves and their every movement so that it matches the forms and lines of classical dance.

Since 1926 many of Dame Ninette's students and dancers have progressed from the Vic-Wells Dancers to the Sadler's Wells Ballet and finally to the Royal Ballet, some of them to become world-famous. Dame Margot Fonteyn, Sir Robert Helpmann and Michael Somes are but a few of those who were responsible for establishing and maintaining the courtly traditions of classical dance at the most testing time of their company's career—when it left Sadler's Wells Theatre and the many provincial theatres of wartime touring to move to the Royal Opera House, Covent Garden. In a theatre of such prestige and before a much larger audience it would have been disastrous if dancers had been intimidated by the new surroundings. That they were not was entirely due to the strict discipline to which they had all submitted. The choice of *The Sleeping Beauty* for the opening night on 20 February 1946 proved, as no other ballet could have done, that classical dance had everything to offer. The Royal Ballet is still at Covent Garden and has yet another production of that favourite classic in its repertory.

Classical dance has developed the most demanding of disciplines. Not all aspirants can master its technique without losing some of the spontaneity and enjoyment shown by children in dance and by primitive and folk dancers. Anthony Dowell is one of the rare classical dancers who communicates his enjoyment in dance yet remains within the principles and rules of classical technique—they have become an integral part of himself and of his total movement. In Dame Ninette's words: 'Classical dance in its purest form is without emotional content or character. Any expression it may show arises through the inspired personality of a dancer who has mastered its technique. It therefore requires freedom to be itself, freedom without tricks or affectation.'

The first thing I considered when attempting a technical book of this kind were illustrations which would reveal the qualities of an artist in movement. The photographs of Anthony Dowell are not intended to be examples of mere technical exactitude. They are, more importantly, an expression of how that pose or step feels in the context of a ballet. They show how the class-room discipline acquires life, quality and colour when performed by an artist who believes in what he is doing.

Anthony Dowell has been through all stages of classical training at the Royal Ballet School and first mastered its principles and rules as they are still taught in the class-room. They then became so much a part of his dance that he no longer had to concentrate on the technicalities, but could set out to master the varying styles of the older ballets in the repertoire, from Perrot's *Giselle* of 1840 to Ashton's many works. His dancing then began to inspire choreographers, particularly Ashton, to create roles specially for him, because his self-discipline, sense of line and, above all, his musicality made him an excellent subject with whom and upon whom to work. His giving of himself to a choreographer and his taking from the choreographer movements with which to fill his personal sphere of dance, and then to communicate their meaning to an audience, have endeared him to many ballet-lovers in many different places. It is sometimes difficult to realise that his imperious Oberon completely commanding the stage and dominating his servant, Puck, and his Queen, Titania, can be the same person who dances the young, slightly gauche Tutor of *A Month in the Country*. Even in the latter role, as a servant of an aristocratic household, he remains in command of the stage because he never loses sight of all those principles that have made him into the great dancer he is.

Perhaps it is more difficult to obtain fitting photographs than readers would imagine. I have danced myself and then taught many on their way to the stage, so that I can feel exactly when a movement is at the point where the photograph must be taken. Such a sense of timing has always been, to me, the outstanding feature of Anthony Crickmay's work. Therefore his willingness to collaborate and experiment to produce the photographs in this book, together with his sympathetic help in selecting the right photograph to reproduce, place me much in his debt, for what he has caught with his camera communicates at a glance what would take me possibly hundreds of words to express. 'But real dance', so Fokine said, 'should have no need of explanations. If it does need words, then the dance and the performer have failed.' Neither Anthony Dowell nor Anthony Crickmay has failed me. I can only express my deepest gratitude for their wonderful sympathy, patience and co-operation.

For their help in researching into the origins of many French terms, I am also deeply indebted to my academic colleagues at the Royal Ballet School, Mademoiselle A. Douchy, Mrs C. Bennett and Peter Davie, who found so much interesting information from the language of the hunt, ancient folklore customs and usage, and the terminology of the French Courts of the seventeenth and eighteenth centuries.

A Definition of Terms

The dancer awakes

'They don't teach you to dance like that now, they only worry about the angle of your head and feet.'

So said a fifteen year old boy student after watching the Anna Pavlova film. It would seem that teachers and students are forgetting the principles of classical dance in their insistence on an exactly detailed performance by every part of the body in any one movement and the constant repetition of a series of limited exercises. As a result, schools are producing technicians geared to one method and syllabus only, instead of dancers capable of adapting their movements to any style of ballet based on classical principles.

But before stating the principles of classical dance it is important to define the meaning of principle, classical, tradition and convention because these terms are constantly used when arguments arise about the merits of this or that method or syllabus. The fullest definitions are given in the Oxford English Dictionary which, in its complete form, is an accepted source for the meaning of English words all over the world. Although from time to time words take on new connotations it is perhaps significant that the meanings of principle and tradition have changed scarcely at all, whereas convention has taken on a further meaning.

Principle

The O.E.D. gives seven definitions of this word, all of which are relevant to the seven principles that govern the performance of classical dance. It is useful to refer to these definitions in order to understand correctly the principles that underlie every movement.

O.E.D. Principle: fundamental source; primary element; fundamental truth as a basis for reasoning; general laws as a guide to action; laws of nature seen in the working of the machine; constituent of some substance, especially giving rise to some quality; personal code of right conduct

---

The human body consists of bones, ligaments, tendons, muscles, nerves, etc., activated by the brain, which can be called the primary element because it is the source of all movement. It is the storehouse of instinctive and acquired knowledge. Its function is to send and receive messages so that every part of the body responds to the command given, to the sense felt.

Every classical dance movement made is limited firstly by the anatomical structure of the individual and secondly by his personal capacity to control all the organs, nerves and muscles with varying degrees of tension and relaxation. These tensions and relaxations change constantly as the line of dance is followed. It is the brain that reasons and directs how the muscles, etc., must be disciplined to move at different lengths and tensions.

If one considers the human body a *machine*, then a study of the anatomy of any boy or girl reveals that each part of the body works in natural relationship to another part as well as to the whole as it moves. From an understanding of this relationship came the principles set down later in this book. But each dancer must also understand his or her own capacity for movement.

Since John Weaver (1723) first explained the relationship of the bones, ligaments, tendons and muscles to each other and to the whole body as it moves, and set down certain basic rules of dance, such important teachers as Noverre, Blasis, Bournonville and Cecchetti have restated the rules and formulated others to be followed by students in all schools no matter by which method or for which syllabus they might study.

Know your own body

But the dancer is not a *machine*. He is a human being and needs to communicate the line and feeling of the movement to others. If, therefore, one dares to call the dancer the *substance* under discussion then it must be said that he must develop some essential *constituents* which will give *quality*, feeling and meaning to the dance. These constituents or attributes are nowhere better described than by Bournonville in his *Etudes Symphoniques* (1861). He demanded from his dancers:

1 A beautiful and supple physique
2 Intelligence used with good taste, imagination and an ability to co-ordinate all parts of the body
3 Artistry and personality
4 Expressiveness and musicality
5 Technical facility

It is perhaps notable that Bournonville gave first and last place to the dancer's physical attributes. If the dancer knows and properly understands the principles that apply to his body when moving, then he must bring all that knowledge and understanding to the performance of steps and poses within the vocabulary of classical movement.

But this is not enough. Bournonville, in his effort to create artists able to express themselves fully with imagination and musicality, demanded much more. He wished dancers to communicate their feelings for the lines of the dance, to phrase their steps to the music and, when necessary, to convey moods, emotions and actions to others. It was not only the principles of classical dance that Bournonville taught. Like all great masters he insisted that his dancers know the rules of stage behaviour, presentation and countless traditional stage practices of the theatre as applied to dance. These had accumulated through generations of teachers, choreographers and dancers.

If the dancer studies all the technical principles and traditional practices, then surely he will have developed a *personal code of right conduct* for the performance of classical or any other form of dance in the theatre.

Tradition

The O.E.D. gives only two meanings for this word, both of which need careful thought. Often what has been retained as a tradition has proved on examination to be merely a continuation of some convention, fashionable at one particular period amongst certain circles of society.

O.E.D. Tradition: opinion or belief in the customs laid down; artistic or literary principles based upon accumulated experience or continual usage

It is because teachers believe so strongly in the methods and class-work of certain dancing-masters that there are many arguments. But today it is more important to examine the reasons behind the methods than to argue about the merits of a

Courtly behaviour

particular syllabus. Agreement must surely be reached that the principles laid down are common to all and that certain traditional practices are most valuable for classical dance.

Since Arbeau (1589) defined in general terms the carriage, behaviour and simple steps of a dancer at court, many later teachers have added to his rules. These relate to stance, turn-out, the balancing of the body over one or two feet, the placing of the parts in relationship to the whole body, to the line of dance, to a partner and, ultimately, to the audience. These principles accumulated by amateurs in the *ballets de cour* were then adopted by professionals dancing in the imperial, royal, state and people's theatres.

As the tastes of audiences changed, so choreographers demanded more and more freedom of movement for their dancers and paid more attention to the qualities of the steps and poses to give them greater expressiveness. They expanded the uses of the body and its relationship to the line of dance, the full dimensions of the stage and to the mood, emotion and action of the ballet. But no matter how much they changed or did away with the rules of courtly behaviour, they never lost sight of the experience of four centuries of dance training. This happened because by constant usage these principles were found to be vital to the development of the dancer's technique.

Today's teachers should understand that without constant attention to the seven principles no dancer can respond to the demands of modern choreographers working in the classical medium.

Convention

O.E.D. Convention: *old meaning* behaviour following tradition; not natural or spontaneous
  new meaning a gathering of people wishing to arrive at an agreed consensus of opinion

Until the beginning of the twentieth century, dancers in royal and state theatres conformed to the strict rules firstly of courtly behaviour and precedence and secondly to those of conventional gesture. But Fokine transformed classical dance into a fully expressive medium by eliminating the conventional rules and gestures, and virtuosity for its own sake, by insisting that dance be the only means of expression no matter in what style, and by suiting the dance to the mood, emotion, theme (or story) and music of each particular ballet. In other words, he eliminated behaviour which reflected the conventions of the court theatres and their aristocratic audiences because they did not appear natural or spontaneous in his ballets—which often reflected the manners and customs of the people.

However much Fokine and other Diaghilev choreographers changed the whole concept of ballet, students in the class-room were never allowed to forget the principles which were inherited from the past masters and which continued to be taught. The only technical difference between the older masters and Fokine (together with his pupil Vaganova) was the latter's insistence that students must co-ordinate their movements exactly to the music.

Since the elimination of the conventions of court and imperial ballets, the term convention has been generally accepted to mean the result of some conference of academicians or teachers about the uses and merits of different methods and syllabuses — provided that there is agreement. But this does not and cannot take into account the way in which dance steps may be used by a choreographer creating a new ballet — or by dancers who have to adapt such movements to the quality and style required in both old and new classical works.

Classicism and Style

Two further definitions should be given if the seven principles of classical dance are to be clearly understood. In the Introduction it was stated that the English school of classical dance is difficult to define. But what does 'classical dance' mean on its own, separated from any discussion of the ballets based on its technical principles and steps? Moreover, what is classicism?

O.E.D. Classicism: following or follower of classical style
    Classical: standard of ancient Greek authors and artists
    Style: the manner of writing, speaking or doing as opposed to the matter expressed or done

---

Classicism in the arts of painting and sculpture signifies an ideal human body. Each work must show a strict sense of balance and formal design, which is serene and generalised rather than individual. In ancient art the human body is portrayed in its most harmonious form, no matter from what angle it is viewed. Thus the lines and angles of head, body, arms and legs must be suitably related to each other and to the central line of balance in order to display a perfectly balanced pose.

Classical style in dance is the vocabulary of movement that conforms to rules established by long practice. The steps and poses from simple folk dances were refined by courtiers and later by dancing-masters who concentrated on how to behave and display oneself to the best advantage in aristocratic society. When professional dancers employed this technique more attention was paid to the look and correct detail of each movement as part of the display. And these movements must show each dancer's body as a perfectly balanced whole.

The choreographer is like a writer, but instead of selecting words appropriate to the meaning and structure of a sentence, he selects steps and poses from the dance vocabulary, phrasing them so that they are appropriate to each other, to the line of dance and to the music. The performers 'who speak his words' must interpret them in the proper style in order to communicate that line of dance to the audience.

The English style retains much of the refinement of courtly behaviour, sense of occasion and elegant line taught by early European dancing-masters. It also reflects elements of the English cultural tradition. During the Commonwealth, John Playford's *The Dancing Master* taught that to dance correctly was to gain entry into a society in which all were equal. In the twentieth century the classical style as taught by Ninette de Valois and adopted by Frederick Ashton reflects the arts of a nation that has concerned itself with the simplicity and forms of Nature—for example, the poems of Shakespeare, Wordsworth and Keats, and the paintings of Constable and Turner. It must be added that although English poets seldom conformed exactly to the academic rules as understood elsewhere in Europe, some were more concerned with the form and manner of writing than with its content.

Ashton's two classical ballets, *Symphonic Variations* and *Scènes de ballet*, reflect aspects of English art. In the former his dance flows onward, revealing the lyrical movements of six dancers weaving continuous patterns. They have come together as equals to enjoy their relationship with each other and with the music. Nothing disturbs the calm spaciousness of their movement. They are there to communicate Ashton's feelings about dance to César Franck's music.

Scènes de ballet is in contrast to *Symphonic Variations*. Like Stravinsky's music to which the scenes are danced, it is concerned with the formal arrangement of phrases within a strictly disciplined pattern. Each phrase has its beginning, climax and end. No detail must be lost—no line of dance smudged. The ballet requires the utmost precision from all. It is led by a soloist, but she must not break away to display her own virtuosity. She is only the focal point in the total picture made by all the dancers.

In other words, both the Ashton ballets are statements about a generalised form of dance, similar to that practised in other European schools, but different from them. English cultural heritage and taste are marked by a preference for simple, clearly stated lyrical forms, rather than for exercises based on the rules and formulas of academicians who are not themselves artists.

A beginning

The Principles of Classical Dance

Stance

Seven essential principles have been formulated by the great masters, from their experience of disciplining the movements of their students within the classical framework. These seven principles are distinct from the seven movements of dance (Noverre 1760), the seven categories of step (Petipa 1890), the five positions of the feet and arms, the five kinds of jump of the old French school, the eight directions of line to be taken and the vocabulary of movement.

Ninette de Valois has said that dancers when performing in a classical ballet must remain within its framework, because a ballet is a general statement about dancing performed by dancers who conform to certain recognised rules. It requires an ordered, balanced form in which calm spaciousness animates the dancers. The seven principles can be briefly summarised as: stance; turn-out; placing; laws of balance; basic rules of the head, legs, arms and body; transfer of weight; and, finally, co-ordination, without which no rule works properly.

I Stance

O.E.D. Stance: position taken; standing correctly

Without the ability to stand and hold himself correctly at all times, the classical dancer has little or no possibility of maintaining turn-out or following the line of dance. He must understand the capacity of his body for movement in this highly disciplined style—and he will get the best results when the spine has been pulled out to its straightest.

1   The tail (coccyx) and pelvis must be pulled downwards and the spine upwards from the waist. The three natural curves of the spine are thereby straightened but must continue to be shock-absorbers as in normal life.

2   The pelvis must be balanced over the two legs and held firmly by the so-called 'muscular corset' with the hips level at all times. The 'corset' consists of all the muscles within the pelvis and of those linking legs to pelvis and pelvis to torso.

3   The torso, from the waist upwards, must be balanced over the pelvis so that the shoulders and hips face the same plane and lie parallel, unless some form of *épaulement* (see page 19) or sideways bend is being used.

4   The rib-cage must be drawn upwards from a slimmed waist. The shoulders are flattened but not pressed on to the rib-cage. The arms are felt to be stretched outwards from the breast-bone in front and from the spine at the back. The lungs can then easily expand and contract sideways with the inhalation and exhalation of breath; and the muscles of the diaphragm and those within the rib-cage can be controlled to support the chest without strain.

5   The legs must be stretched away from the hip-joints into the feet, so that the body's weight rests firmly over the three points of balance: the big and little toes, and the heel.

6   The head must be held erect so that the crown is directly over the insteps of the two unturned-out feet. The eyes must look outwards. Breathing should be deep and steady. *No tension should be felt anywhere.*

II Turn-out

O.E.D. Turn-out: rotary motion; bringing to view

'The "turn-out" is an absolute necessity if the dancer aims at the perfection of a purely classical line.' (Ninette de Valois). Its achievement requires an understanding of muscle-control within the thighs, pelvis, legs and stomach in order to maintain correct placing.

1   The turn-out must take place within the hip-joints; the knees and thighs are rotated outwards as far as possible so that the feet turn out.

2   Each knee must be kept in a natural relationship to the line of its leg and foot. Thus it will always be directly in line with the centre of the pelvis whether it faces forwards or (when turned out) sideways and whether the leg is bent or straight.

3   Each foot must bend straight upwards or stretch straight downwards from the ankle towards and away from the centre of the knee; thus the foot will only work at right angles to the lower leg and knee and must not roll inwards or sickle outwards at the ankle (see page 27).

If these rules are at all times applied correctly, they prevent the weight from coming too far back on the heels.

Although de Valois's remark stressed the importance of perfect turn-out, she added a valuable comment for dancers who find its achievement difficult: 'It is better to sacrifice some part of the turn-out than lose the line and quality of a movement and the symmetry of a pose. It is far more important to maintain the natural relationship of the parts to the whole leg when drawing the line of dance.'

Bring to view

III Placing

Placing in classical dance can be discussed under three headings, all of which are vital to the creation of a proper line of movement.

Placing

O.E.D. Placing: arranging things in their proper place to achieve an ordered, balanced form

---

'Movement made by any dancer can be symmetrical or asymmetrical. In pure classical dance symmetry is demanded. It does not take into account the effect that emotion, mood or personal characteristics can have on the dancer's body to upset its equilibrium.' (Ninette de Valois)

Symmetry

The body is basically symmetrical. The arms and legs weigh equally on each side. The crown of the head is centred directly over the spine and feet. The weight of the body is thus evenly balanced over the feet (the base). Turn-out once achieved, the head and torso must remain properly centred over this base even when it changes shape as weight is transferred to one foot or even more as the dancer rises through the foot to the full *pointe*.

In order to keep the head and body correctly placed in relation to the legs, the spine must not be stiffened. Its natural curves, from the waist upwards, must always act as shock-absorbers as they do normally. They must allow the dancer to adjust his balance to every change of weight as he draws the line of dance by steps and poses.

Asymmetry

Four rules are helpful to the mastery of this first kind of placing:

1 Each part of the body must be kept in natural relationship to the others and to the centre line of balance.

2 An arm or leg should never be allowed to over- or under-cross the centre line of the body.

3 The head, the heaviest part of the body, must always lead the movement. The foot or feet must always follow the head. The head never follows the feet. In other words, the head always anticipates the line of movement and the direction to be taken.

4 The arms must never fall behind the shoulders. If they do, the weight will be too far back.

Correct relationships

Placing Also Means Alignment

O.E.D. Alignment: bringing into line; especially bringing three or more points into line

In dance, alignment means bringing the head, body, arms and legs into ever-changing line with the stage and audience.

'Some dancers have a natural sense of line, but the sense of drawing lines in movement and controlling them in repose must be cultivated by studying the principles of alignment.' (Ninette de Valois)

The dancer tries to imagine himself as the centre of a square drawn on the floor. One side of it lies along the front of the stage. If the dancer faces that side, he directly faces the audience or is, in other words, *de face*.

The square is divided by eight lines radiating from the dancer's central point of balance. Each position (step or pose) must be directed outwards along one of the eight lines. The square is personal to each dancer and, as each movement is made, the square moves with him and the lines have to be redrawn to fill the stage.

Although the term 'square' is widely used, it is incorrect because the dancer moves through space, through many dimensions. The movements made by the legs are joined to each other and co-ordinated with the carriage of the head, arms and torso as they travel through some part of a circle. (N.B. The arms are always rounded except in *arabesque*. See page 30.) The total movement is made within a cube or sphere which gives height, breadth, depth and length to the flow of line within the choreographic design.

The Italian school of Blasis contributed most to the study of alignment and the understanding of appropriate head movements. Blasis numbered the eight points of the square and set down how the dancer must align each part of the body correctly for every step and pose. It is the relationship of the hips, shoulders and working leg to one point in the personal square that directs the dancer to a correct alignment.

The numbered square is only significant as a beginning. Today a broader view has to be taken. Since Fokine first enlarged the dancer's range of expressive movement, others, notably Ashton and Robbins, have further developed the scope of the classical dancer.

Placing Also Means *Epaulement*

Too often the word 'alignment' is used when *épaulement* is intended—and *épaulement* is not the same thing. The meaning found in French dictionaries is mainly concerned with military defence: 'a protective wall built at an angle to withstand an enemy'—derived from *épaule*, a shoulder, *épauler*, to shoulder (a musket, etc.).

Alignment

Epaulement

However, the best definition of *épaulement* in classical dance was given by Peter Davie, teacher of French at the Royal Ballet School: 'A rotary movement of the shoulders made in sympathy with a simultaneous movement of the arms and/or legs, the extent of which must be finely judged, but which will depend on the context. It really is a state of mind.'

Since Filippo Taglioni created a romantic style of classical dance for his daughter, Marie Taglioni, with which to give expression to the moods, emotions and actions of her famous role in *La Sylphide*, the French, Danes and Russians have adopted a slight and subtle turn of the body from the waist upwards. This 'shading' or 'shouldering' of a *port de bras* gives a softer more flowing line than the purely classical placing of the head and arms in the correct alignment which insists that the hips and shoulders must always be level and face the same direction. To achieve this subtle 'shading' the dancer must allow the head and arms to move freely and easily. He must also have great flexibility from the waist upwards. By the elimination of tension, this subtle 'shading' will appear to be the natural outcome of torso and legs in co-ordination as the dancer draws the lines of dance through space.

IV The Laws of Balance

O.E.D. Balance: a counterpoise (of things) in order to maintain equilibrium

---

There are only two laws of balance to remember. They should be applied appropriately as the dancer follows the line of dance and conforms to the other basic rules.

1 The Law of Opposition

Whether working or supporting, the leg in front should be balanced by the opposite arm coming forwards. The dancer must be in correct alignment (see page 19) with hips and shoulders level and lying parallel to each other, facing the same plane and directed to one point in the personal square.

2 The Law of *Epaulement*

Whether working or supporting, the leg in front should be matched by the forward movement of the same shoulder. This law is more usually followed when a movement is to be 'shaded' as in *épaulement* (see page 19). Dancers should study this law carefully, in relationship to stance, turn-out and placing in its first form (see page 16).

Law of opposition

Counterpoise

The following comments by Ninette de Valois should also be carefully studied because they make important points about balancing over one or both feet.

'The dancer must determine the relationship of the arms and legs to the central point of balance and see that the law of opposition or *épaulement* used is logical. Is the weight correctly centred? Are the legs and arms so counter-balanced that they help equalise the pressure of weight on the supporting leg (legs)? Does this position help the dancer to remain calm? Is it easy to move from that step or pose to another as the weight is transferred without twisting some part of the body and thus spoiling the line of movement?'

The weight must be evenly distributed throughout the body, particularly for poses such as *attitude* and *arabesque*. In these poses the pelvis must tilt (or bow) over the supporting leg as the working leg is raised or stretched behind, the lower spine elongated and the upper spine stretched and curved backwards towards the centre of the body. The head needs a further stretch upwards and usually a little backwards if it is to play its proper part in balancing the total line of the *arabesque* over the supporting leg. The arms add to the total line of the *arabesque* only by complementing this line (see page 30).

The middle of the body (i.e. the centre of the waist) is the central point of the dancer's personal sphere or cube (see page 19). The legs and arms are directed outwards from this centre, the tips of the fingers and toes being the extreme limit of those lines running diagonally through the centre of the body in two directions. The arms and legs must therefore be lowered or raised in relationship to the movements made outwards from the centre if the sphere is to be properly filled with dance.

The pull between the opposing forces of arms and legs helps the dancer to maintain balance. But to achieve this, the dancer must make a strong movement with the arms so that they begin and finish with the movement of the legs. The arms must also be used to balance the body after a *pirouette* or on landing from a jump, particularly where a change of direction or turn has been made or will have to be made in the next step.

A most important rule for dancing in *adage* is: 'Get into a position and hold it!' It is also important for a jump or *pirouette*. The step should end with the dancer holding the pose. This can only happen if the foot or feet work correctly as the base, and weight is correctly balanced over that base.

Through the centre

V The Basic Rules of Classical Technique

O.E.D. Rule: dominant custom; canon; test; normal state of things

'It is better to have a rule to break than no rules at all if chaos is not to reign in the class-room and on the stage.' (Ninette de Valois)

Although an attempt can be made to set down rules for each part of the body, no one rule can be practised for itself alone. As with the seven movements of dance (to bend, stretch, rise, jump, glide, dart and turn—Noverre 1760), they cannot be discussed in isolation. The anatomical structure of the body is such that when one part of the body is used or one movement made, some muscles work in one way and some in another, counterpoising each other to help the dancer maintain balance. For example, in order to bend the legs in *plié* some muscles relax, others stretch; or, in order to stretch the leg in *développé*, some muscles stretch and others raise the leg into position.

1 The Rules of the Head

1   The head leads the movement and is always in control. The eyes must be trained to find the direction to be followed before the movement begins because, without training, the eyes will instinctively look straight ahead even when the movement is sideways.

2   The head must always move freely and independently of the neck and torso, allowing no twist of the shoulders to throw the body out of alignment (see page 19). It must also move freely for *épaulement*, for otherwise the eyes will not find the direction to be followed, particularly if some turn is involved.

3   In turns or *pirouettes* the eyes must focus to the front, or point at which the turn will begin and end, before the dancer starts to move. However, there are exceptions to this rule if the turn or *pirouette* has to end at a different point. In such cases the head has to work quickly to find the new point and to be so accurate that the dancer maintains balance.

4   Every change of alignment and *épaulement* must be seen by the audience. The head leads the change and helps the dancer to travel in the correct direction the moment that the movement begins.

2 The Rules of the Legs and Feet

1   The dancer must know the feeling of a fully stretched leg. This allows him to control the spacing of movement. It is particularly important when a child is growing because the length of leg at any time should determine the length of step to be taken when transferring from one leg to the other. The student should

Croisé devant

understand when to use a small or large 2nd or 4th position. The small position is usually taken when moving from straight legs or from a *demi-plié* without using a fully stretched working leg (as in a *chassé*). The large position is taken when moving from a *demi-plié* or *fondu* with a fully stretched working leg—as it then moves much more easily. A small position is usually better for *pirouettes en dehors* and a large one for *pirouettes en dedans*.

2   The floor (which plays an important part in dance) is not a resting place. It is used as a spring-board to stimulate the muscles under the foot and those of the legs. The dancer must not sit in a *plié* or *fondu* before or after any movement and, since all rises, *relevés* and jumps begin and end with a *plié* or *fondu*, every dancer must learn how to perform and use these two movements correctly.

3   The toe, the extreme part of the leg and the first to return to the floor after a step, will not leave the floor with sufficient impetus for any *battement*, rise, *relevé* or jump if the whole foot, particularly the heel, has not been pressed into the floor at the beginning of the movement and then at its end. It is the weight of the body pressing down through the bones of the leg on to the foot (or feet) that causes the muscles under the instep instantaneously to expand and contract. This action and reaction propels the whole body into the air and holds it firmly when it returns to the floor.

4   Fully to understand the impetus given by the foot and leg to any step, the dancer must be able to feel and control the movement as it passes through the centre of the leg and the three parts of the foot, i.e. the quarter, half and three-quarter *pointes*. The rise and fall of this movement through the foot is particularly important for steps of *élévation sur place*, because the feet must work twice as hard if height is to be gained. It is the controlled and constant contraction and expansion of the muscles under the foot, caused by the pressure of weight from the body as it falls, rises and falls again, that gives the dancer that strength and firm base to begin and then to hold the end of each step.

5   As a dancer gains speed, the space filled by a step becomes less. Therefore the leg must be used as economically as possible—but with the same quality, accuracy and style. In order to find the most direct and simple way to perform a step, dancers must never lose sight of the above rules and the placing of the steps. They must always be aware of the direction into which they have to step, jump, beat or turn and move exactly towards or at that point and nowhere else. To do all this it is very useful not only to use one of the three points of balance of the foot with accuracy, but also to decide upon the exact degree of *plié* to give the best results. A quarter *plié* may be better than a full *demi-plié* when working at speed, particularly if the dancer naturally possesses a very deep *demi-plié*.

6   The angle at which the fully stretched leg is held on departure from the floor determines the line drawn in any jump with feet apart—therefore the height of the leg from the floor must always be controlled so that the line drawn reaches its proper conclusion.

In addition, the dancer should maintain the same relationship between the legs whether the supporting leg is bent, straight or poised *sur la pointe*. If this is not done, some part of the line or quality of the movement will be lost. For it is often the height and relationship of a dancer's head and body to the floor pattern which bring out the essential contrasts to be made between steps, e.g. a step which is *élancé* (darted) as opposed to one which is *sauté* (jumped) or *glissé* (glided).

7   A vital quality of any jump is its lightness. The dancer must determine the correct emphasis to give to a particular step in order to keep it light. Too heavy a preparation or finish will destroy that quality. For this reason, the dancer usually has to change into a downward accent or to emphasise into an upward one. Since this contrasting of one step with another contributes so much to the spaciousness of classical dance, dancers must learn not only how to keep their legs in proper relationship but how to control the emphasis made so that it gives the correct impetus to a movement.

8   Work must also be kept light to gain speed. This is specially important in *pointe* work, where the axiom, in Ninette de Valois's words, is: 'Keep off your *pointes*, when you are on them, by moving fast. *Pointe* work must be silent.' This is the most important rule and must always be kept in mind. Petipa stated: '*Pointes* are the finishing touch to the women's side of classical dance. They are not the sole reason for the ballet.'

Ninette de Valois adds: 'If the dancer can control the height and angle of the working leg and the accent or emphasis to be made in all *pointe* work, it will give strength to the back. And if the spine is correctly centred with each movement, she will be able to keep her weight off her *pointes*. This will lend speed to her steps and speed in most *pointe* work is essential. Speed and neatness must never be sacrificed for space.'

3   The Rules of the Arms

'Style is conveyed through the *ports de bras* of classical dance because it is within the *ports de bras* that it is first possible to distinguish the subtle differences to be made between a classical, a romantic and a modern ballet if these are based on the academic rules and technique. Style represents the march of time.' (Ninette de Valois)

But the arms do not only convey style. They are the framework to the head and torso. They play a vital part in conveying expression and meaning. Without sensitive hands and arms the dancer is dumb.

1   The classical *ports de bras* are performed within their own sphere (see page 19). The hands begin some four to six inches away from the lower half of the body (i.e. *bras bas*) and then are raised to a point some four to six inches away from the eyes and above the head (i.e. 5th). From there they are opened and lowered sideways through 2nd position to the starting point. All other positions are to be found within this sphere except those for *arabesques*, where the straightening of the elbow and turning of the wrist will stretch the hand and fingers beyond the sphere.

2   The natural flow of the arms should be used to bring life to the *ports de bras*. This flow is best understood when the dancer feels the weight of the arm being carried

Classical *port de bras*

upwards or downwards, inwards or outwards, feels the stretch of the arm following a circular line and feels the movement part of a continuous curve. To feel this he should realise that there are four lines along which to exert the pressure necessary to move against the air. And while realising this, the dancer must think of the whole arm moving freely within its socket, in order to achieve the fullest extension permitted in classical dance (see 4b below).

3   The fundamental rules of the classical *ports de bras* must never be ignored as they give breadth and balance to each movement. Correctly performed they contribute to the vital flow and line of the dance.

4   A simple *port de bras* is always to be preferred in class-work. 'Choreography begins when the choreographer substitutes an unorthodox movement for the conventional one.' (Ninette de Valois)

The simplest and most useful *ports de bras* are those based on the already stated rules and the following:

a   The arms must never move behind the body except in *arabesque*.

b   The arms must always be rounded except in *arabesque*. They must never touch the body.

c   In 1st position the finger-tips are level with the bottom of the breast bone.

d   When opening outwards into 2nd position, the arms must always follow the shoulder-line downwards. In other words, if the arms move directly outwards from 1st, they must not be raised or lowered. This outward movement is round the circumference of a horizontal circle within the personal sphere (see 1 above).

e   When arms are in 5th position, the head erect and the eyes slightly raised, the woman dancer can look into the palms of her hands, the man see his little fingers. The shoulders must be held down and wide and easy. The upward movement into 5th is round the circumference of a vertical circle.

f   A valuable but conventional rule of all older schools is that every time the dancer changes weight from one foot to the other through one of the five positions, the arms have to go through 1st position to stabilise the body at the moment of transfer. In the early stages of training this rule is still the most important. At a later stage the dancer must see that the *port de bras* used does help to control the body and the dancer to maintain balance.

g   All *ports de bras* must be kept calm, particularly in *pointe* work where emphasis lies in the use of the feet and legs. If the *ports de bras* are to be calm, they must be exact and economical—and they are therefore better simple.

h   The hand, like the arm, must appear calm, but alive whenever the dancer pauses momentarily in some pose or at the point of greatest effort, because each movement must be felt right through the body from the head to the tips of fingers and toes.

It is unwise to break away from the formal aspect of the classical *ports de bras* when wearing a tutu, that most revealing of garments, whose very shape demands careful attention to the exact details of calm yet spacious movement. The fact that the

A deux bras

shoulders are so often uncovered can reveal any misplaced movement, but can also disclose the full line of the arm as it describes a beautiful curve and falls downwards from 5th to 2nd position.

Yet the *ports de bras* of the older classical schools can be altered to become romantic or modern: romantic by using the softer flow of the arms; modern by a straightening and lengthening of the total movement, or by a bending or twisting of some part of the arms to give a more angular or athletic effect.

Fokine said: 'To dance in the romantic style means to be classical from the feet to the waist, but from the waist upwards the body, head and arms must have freedom to express themselves within the content, mood and emotions of the plot.'

Similarly, to dance in the *demi-caractère* style means to be classical from the feet to the waist, but thence upwards the body, head and arms must have freedom to express the character played and the action of the plot.

Every dancer must therefore make a clear but subtle distinction between the romantic and *demi-caractère ports de bras*. Without this distinction, the arms soon begin to be exaggerated and to lose their significance.

4   The Rules of the Body

Whereas in most forms of dance the torso can be said to begin at the coccyx and hip-joints, in classical dance this is not so. In classical dance the torso commences at the waist-line with a very occasional movement below (in an *arabesque* the pelvis tilts forwards). The need for stillness in the pelvic girdle is essential if the turn-out is to be maintained (see page 14). The pelvic girdle encased in the 'muscular corset' must be kept balanced over the turned-out legs and must be kept as still as possible if the hips are to remain level (see page 13). But the torso from the waist upwards must be balanced over the pelvis if the dancer is to maintain and control the line it makes as weight is transferred through the centre line of balance and as the movements flow from one to another (see page 39). For this reason the torso upwards from the waist must never be held stiffly. It must be in a state of tonicity, that is, always in a state of readiness to respond to the demands of flow of line.

It is important to follow the rules given below if the flexibility of the classical torso is to be understood.

1   When using alignment (see page 19) the hips and shoulders must always face the same plane and be level, thus lying parallel to each other except in *arabesques*. In these poses the need to stabilise the balance over the supporting leg and a very narrow base with the pelvis tilted forwards at a greater or lesser angle means that the hip of the raised leg will be tilted very slightly upwards and backwards. However, if the dancer has stretched the leg fully away from the hip socket, that slight but necessary adjustment is scarcely noticeable, particularly if the upper spine and head are also stretched upwards and backwards towards the centre line of balance (see page 18).

Romantic *port de bras*

Demi-caractère port de bras

Modern *port de bras*

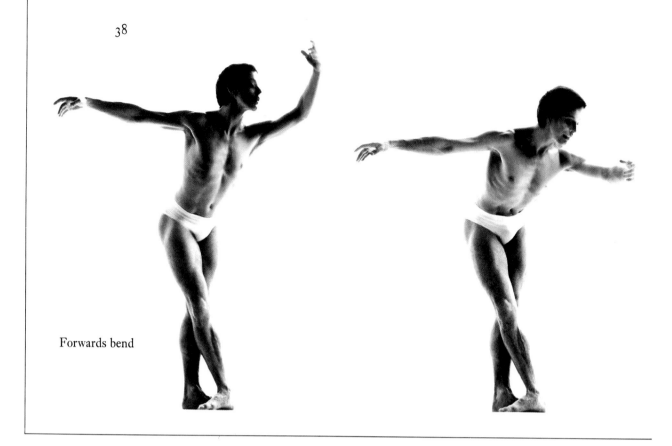

Forwards bend

2   When using *épaulement* (see page 19) the hips will be level and facing the plane to
     which the movement is directed, but from the waist upwards the torso will be
     turned slightly forwards or backwards from that plane. 'The dancer must think
     of the *épaulement* with the head and shoulders.' (Ninette de Valois)

3   The arms must move freely in their sockets if the dancer is to balance the torso
     over the pelvic girdle. The shoulders must not be pressed downwards nor
     inwards on to the rib-cage or spine. Similarly the head must be allowed to move
     independently of the spine. Whenever the torso curves widely outwards from the
     centre line of balance, the head, being the heaviest part of the body, must direct
     the line of movement and act to balance the weight of the torso. The head always
     endeavours to keep above or towards the central line so that its weight, if
     displaced, will not throw the dancer off balance. The head always tries
     instinctively to retain equilibrium.

4   Nothing must be allowed to impede the action of all the respiratory muscles
     which cover a wide area of the torso. The lungs must be free to expand and
     contract easily as the dancer times the exhalation and inhalation (see page 13) in
     order to synchronise the breath with the effort (e.g. a rise into a *pirouette* or
     jump). The chest should not be held rigidly or too far upwards as this only
     throws the weight too far back and leads to shallow breathing which destroys the
     calm of the classical line. The arms must be held away from the body and, as
     already stated, on no account must the shoulder-blades rest heavily on the rib-
     cage or spine.

5　It is most important that each dancer understand and use the curves of the spine to the limit. These curves are at the neck (cervical), the chest (thoracic) and from above the waist. In pure classical dance there should be no curving forwards, sideways or backwards below the waist, although the great spinal and abdominal muscles in the pelvic girdle will play some part in any bending movement. Nevertheless it must be clear that the pelvic girdle should only tilt forwards in a straight line to a greater or lesser degree. No matter at which angle the pelvis is held, the torso should only curve forwards, sideways or backwards from the waist upwards.

VI　Transfer of Weight

O.E.D. Transfer: to convey or hand over one thing or person to another place or person

When transferring weight from one foot to the other, the dancer must be sure that the entire body goes over to the new supporting leg through the centre line of balance; therefore adjustments have to be made throughout the whole body, even if only minimal ones.

Soubresaut

The legs must be controlled at all times if the flow of movement is to be maintained. The dancer must be able to feel the fully stretched leg from hip to toe and appreciate the swift, accurate transfer of weight needed to reverse the functions of a supporting leg and a working leg. This change takes place even in the slightest movement from a 1st to a 5th position of the feet, using a *battement tendu* or small *retiré*. If the change is not accurate the dancer cannot move smoothly nor maintain speed. Also, it is not possible for him to achieve that delicacy of movement which demands that no jerk and no unequal gaps be seen between the legs, particularly in such steps as *pas de bourrée courus* or *suivis*.

Yet the dancer should never be afraid of too wide a position when transferring weight as it lends spaciousness to the dance when this is needed. It always helps to stretch a dancer who is tight or not generous in movement. The dancer should be in control of the space covered, and should always be able to extend or lessen the amount of space.

The Use of the Five Positions of the Feet

The first ballet-master systematically to define the five positions of the feet and their uses was Beauchamps (1702). His analysis decreed that they are those positions where both feet are firmly placed on the floor. No matter what their relationship to each other, whether they are apart or close together, they have the weight of the body directly centred above them.

Very much later the old French school defined the five positions of the arms which were used simultaneously with those of the feet. Just before, during and after the transfer both arms and feet would move through 1st position, e.g. from 4th *croisé devant* through 1st and then into 2nd position.

This formal transfer of weight is no longer so firmly upheld. Nevertheless it is notable that even in today's highly complicated choreography, the dancer's ability to recover balance after some particularly difficult turn or bend of the body comes only from understanding the rule that any transfer of weight must be felt to go through the centre line of balance. The best way to accomplish this movement is the firm placing of the feet in one of the five positions at the moment of transfer—unless the dancer is on one leg only, as in *adage*, or has to transfer weight during a jump.

The Five Jumps

There are five jumps of different kinds and it is not always understood that in three of these the weight of the body must be transferred through the centre of balance whilst the dancer is in the air. This can only happen if the correct impetus is given to the preparation into and out of the floor, and if the body and legs are held still at the height of the jump. This 'hold' in the air and in the transfer determines the line to be drawn and ensures that the jump will be completed with the weight firmly fixed over one foot or both feet.

The five jumps and the impetus required to propel the dancer into the air are as follows:

1   *From two feet to two feet*, e.g. *changements de pieds*
    The impetus comes from both feet pressing into and out of the floor, the weight of the body being kept absolutely centred from the beginning to the end of the jump. If the dancer has to travel in any direction during a *soubresaut*, the head should be directed the way it should travel. It is usual for the torso similarly to anticipate the line to be followed.

2   *From two feet to one foot*, e.g. *sissonnes*
    The impetus must come from both feet. At the height of the jump the weight of the body must be centred over the foot upon which the dancer will descend. In a *sissonne ordinaire sur place* from 5th position, it is sufficient to jump straight upwards and to lift the working foot to the required height from the floor just before the toes of both feet reach the floor. If the distance to be travelled in a *sissonne ouverte* is not far, it is usually sufficient to think of the distance and direction to be travelled and to allow the head to lead the movement. However, if the distance is far, then the head must lead the whole line of the body appropriately onwards as both feet press into and out of the floor in that direction. At the height of the jump the weight must be centred and held over what will be the supporting leg on landing, particularly if the final pose has to be held. This has special importance when the dancer has to hold the working leg either in 4th position *devant* at 90° or any *arabesque*. It is essential to hold any pose at the height of the jump and to maintain that pose when landing.

Sissonne écartée

3 *From one foot to two feet*, e.g. *assemblés*

It is important to decide whether the *assemblé* is to be travelled or *en place*. If it is to be *en place*, then the impetus is first given to the working foot as it glides outwards, the weight being held firmly over the supporting leg. The moment the toe is about the leave the floor, the dancer must press and spring upwards from the supporting leg. At the height of the jump, he must join both legs together and descend directly downwards on to the same spot at which the jump began.

If, on the other hand, the *assemblé* is to be travelled, the movement commences as above but the working foot must give greater impetus, the toe leaving the floor just before the dancer springs upwards and towards the point indicated by the working toe. The dancer then presses upwards and towards that point. At the height of this jump, the weight must be re-centred over the two legs as they join together in the air so that the dancer descends on both feet equally.

Assemblé écarté

4   *From one foot to the other*, e.g. all kinds of *jetés*

When jumping from two feet to one, or one foot to two, the weight must be stabilised at the height of the jump exactly over the centre of the foot upon which the dancer has to land. However, when jumping from one foot to the other, the weight must be stabilised and exactly centred over the two legs whilst in the air at the height of the jump. The dancer must do this whether he has one or both legs straight or bent. As *jetés* are so varied, it is essential that the dancer understand which is the highest point, as the following examples demonstrate.

Petits jetés en place, or slightly travelling

The dancer should give the same impetus as for *assemblé en place*, but push more strongly upwards and at the height of the jump bring the raised leg backwards and under the body so that the transfer takes place in the air. The dancer will then descend firmly on to the new supporting leg without displacing his weight.

Grand jeté en avant

The purely classical *grand jeté en avant* describes an upward curving line before descending, the impetus being given by the pressure of the supporting leg into and out of the floor as the working leg rises in a *grand battement devant*. At this moment the body curves slightly backwards so that the head is just behind the jump. Then, as the dancer reaches the height of the jump, the legs are equally stretched outwards and at the same height from the floor, the head and body stretched exactly between them. The dancer then travels forwards and downwards to the point indicated by the leading toe and lands in *arabesque fondue* because the pose has been anticipated and held from the beginning of the jump.

This same action of the head, body and legs takes place in *grand jeté élancé*, except that the spine is not curved so far backwards as the pose taken is usually an open *attitude*. This pose facilitates the change in the line of dance and must take place just as the greatest height is reached (see page 57). This 'hold' of the body absolutely still at the height of a jump in *arabesque* or *attitude* is vital in all double-work for it is at this moment that the boy must catch and hold the girl.

The 'split' or 'flick' *jeté* should find the dancer's weight more or less centred throughout the jump, the head and body helping to propel the dancer onwards, usually at speed. It is rare that a pose has to be held on completion of such *jetés*, but if an *arabesque* is required, then, as the supporting leg descends into *fondue*, the body must simultaneously stretch outwards and upwards with the working leg into the proper *arabesque* line. The dancer should feel on landing that he is 'stretched in half', as happens after the classical *grand jeté en avant*.

Grand jeté en tournant

The *grand jeté en tournant* is the most difficult of jumps to perform and time exactly because the highest point, as seen from the audience, is when the dancer has risen with the *grand battement devant*, arms in 5th position. But films of the movement show that the distance of the legs from the floor increases as the dancer makes the swift half-turn in the air and as he opens the arms to 2nd or another position while curving the body slightly backwards ready to descend into an *arabesque*. Performed exactly, the dancer appears to hover in the air for a moment.

Grand jeté en avant

5   *All on one leg*, e.g. *temps levés, fouettés sautés*

Because the weight is already centred over one leg and the dancer remains *en place* during these jumps, all that is necessary is to keep the weight correctly centred over that leg in the appropriate pose. The body can be held in *arabesque*, the pelvis tilted and held forwards, or in a *grand pose devant* at 90° with the body stretched slightly backwards. The same applies if the dancer has to travel in some direction or other, or is dancing *cabrioles* where some impetus is often given by a preliminary *pas marché* or *chassé* before the spring upwards from the supporting leg.

However, if the dancer is to perform *grand fouetté sauté* then the same rule applies as for *grand jeté en tournant*. The dancer must give a simultaneous strong impetus upwards from both the supporting leg and the arms when performing the *grand battement sauté devant* and swiftly change the alignment at the height of the jump (see page 69). It will be found that if the dancer follows the rules of alignment and makes an absolutely clear change of direction in the air when moving *en dehors*, or more rarely *en dedans*, it will be much easier to descend in the final pose. When using this step the dancer must decide exactly what the final pose is to be. The purely classical *grand fouetté sauté* demands that a clean half-turn be made. Nevertheless, in *Giselle* the Wilis should use the romantic form since they are conforming to the law of *épaulement* (see page 19) and are shading their movements. The body is slightly turned towards the raised leg and the head looks under the raised arm after little more than a quarter turn in the air.

VII Co-ordination

O.E.D. Co-ordinate: to bring parts into proper relationship

The seventh and most vital principle of classical dance is co-ordination, without which no step can become part of dance. It was when discussing the need to co-ordinate all parts of the body that Noverre defined the seven movements of dance in his *Letters on Dance* (1760).

'Accuracy in classical dance is what matters and if there is to be accuracy then there must be unity and discipline. Only then will there be co-ordination.'

Ninette de Valois's words sum up exactly what is required from the dancer because there must be a total response from all parts of the body if they are to move in harmony with the line of dance and the music.

Temps levé

The arms and hands must always be alive and synchronise exactly with the legs and feet so that they begin together and arrive simultaneously at the finished position. They complete the full expressiveness of a pose or movement. They are vital elements communicating emotional significance and meaning to all forms of dance. But they must be controlled if they are to achieve that symmetry and placing demanded in classical dance (see page 16). They must be controlled if they are to take part appropriately in every movement, to supply impetus and accent, and always to follow the line visualised by the head and eyes.

Flow of line can be likened to the melody and like the melody it must have its rhythm, its rises and falls, its diminuendos and accelerandos, its pianissimos and fortissimos. Flow of line is the most musical element in dance, continuously carrying the dancer onwards in time as well as space. An *enchaînement*, like the line of a song, must be so phrased that its climax, the high-point or pose, appears to be the logical outcome of what has gone before and in fact arises from the careful weaving of the movement from the beginning to the climax and end.

It is the changes that the dancer makes in the rhythmic flow of each *enchaînement* which ensure a proper development not only within the dance context but also, in a ballet with a story, of the action and character. When determining the rhythmic flow of line in any *enchaînement*, dance or ballet, the dancer must take into account several vital musical factors which can be broadly defined as melody, time, tempo, rhythm and phrasing. To do this the dancer must concentrate on the quality of each step and pose, and draw attention to the contrasts between the various movements. Yet he must keep these contrasts within the framework of the style and context of the *enchaînement*.

Once the dancer has mastered the first simple exercises which give an understanding of the basic principles of classical dance, he must begin to understand and use appropriately the seven movements as stated by Noverre, as well as the seven categories of step as visualised by Petipa (see page 65 *et seq*). He must then concentrate on the quality of each step in relationship to the others within the *enchaînement*. Whilst making the necessary contrasts he must keep within the framework of the particular phrasing being danced. Is it danced during an *adage*, a *petit allegro* or *grand allegro*, or other musical context and tempo? Whatever the *enchaînement*, it should never over-complicate the flow of line, because this will allow the dancer too little time in which to fulfil, or develop if need be, every movement in detail, in which case the phrasing will not be smooth or easy to perform.

Both teachers and dancers should study how to join the various movements together so that they are compatible and well phrased, for it is the dancer's ability to phrase correctly that is the ultimate secret of classical dance. He must phrase the steps and poses so that they become rhythmically alive and in harmony with the music, or acquire a rhythm of their own which the music must follow.

The late Frank Howes who, more than any critic of his day, understood and loved ballets based on classical technique, once explained how classical dance, which is by nature silent, should become musically and rhythmically alive. He wrote: 'Dance rhythm means the particular organisation of movement in time, space and intensity through the grouping of various types of poses and steps. Large overall patterns can be created and within them shorter phrase rhythms. But the basis of them all is that they exist as groups and by being efficient in action and appropriate to the context and/or music give pleasure to both performer and onlooker.'

The Seven Movements of Dance

When in 1723 Weaver defined his four movements of dance he was analysing the four movements of which the body is capable, i.e. to bend, stretch, rise or raise, turn or rotate. In 1760, Noverre defined his seven movements in terms of quality of the steps his dancers had to perform. Many teachers and dancers today think only of what the legs perform and forget that the whole body is involved. An attempt must be made to clarify the meaning of Noverre's seven movements.

In 1702 Beauchamps and his pupil Feuillet had first named and written down steps for dances basically designed for the more educated courtiers of the period, steps which were a great deal simpler than those of today. (Yet the quality of these early steps remains the same in the hands of a great choreographer.) Names were given according to the basic French meaning and usage laid down by the first members of the Académie Française in 1584.

As the French and oldest form of dance training travelled, so other nationalities adopted the words spoken by their teachers without comprehending their exact meaning or use. Since the sixteenth century there has been little or no change in the basic French meaning and usage of the terms still employed. So it is helpful to refer to the Larousse and Cassell (French-English) dictionaries in order to define what Noverre meant by his seven movements.

---

1   *Plier :* to bend; fold; or fold up

Even the simplest *plié* needs the co-ordination of legs, arms and head if it is to be a dancing movement and to create a flow of line. It is the first exercise to be studied in class.

The legs are bent at three points until the *demi-plié* position is reached and at four from there to the full *plié*. In other words, the dancer bends the legs at the hip-joints, knees and ankles—and finally the feet at the metatarsal arches.

The dancer's arms are always curved except in *arabesque*, which means that they are bent at the arm-socket, elbow, wrist and fingers. The head can also bend or curve forwards, sideways or backwards. The spine alone remains stretched and still though it, too, can fold up, as it were, when the dancer sinks to the floor through a *plié*—as does Odette in *Swan Lake* as she alights at the Prince's feet.

To bend

To stretch

2   *Etendre*: to stretch; or spread

The second exercise to be studied is usually *battement tendu*, the working leg stretching throughout its length from hip to toe outwards from a closed position. The legs must also be fully stretched, but upwards, in order to regain stance after any *plié*.

The arm is fully stretched outwards from its socket only in *arabesque*, but should be stretched within the curve if arms, like legs, are to move freely.

If the spine is not stretched to its fullest when the dancer is standing in any of the five positions of the feet, then stance is not correct. After any movement when the body has been bent, the spine must be stretched again in order to regain height.

But there is also the idea of spreading, the feeling a dancer should have when breathing deeply and stretching arms widely away from the body to give breadth, depth and height to the line of dance as it flows on. This is particularly important in such movements as *développés*, where only one leg works, and in *battements fondus*, where there must be visible equality of movement in both legs although one is working and the other supporting.

The arms play a vital part in these movements, together with inclinations or turns of the head which not only help to keep the dancer on balance but are part of the flow of line. They are part of the breadth of movement which expresses the dancer's ability and desire to give generously and thereby to convey meaning.

The action of bending then stretching, accompanied by the feeling of spreading outwards, has to be practised constantly if there is to be a smooth transition from one movement to another.

3   *Relever*: to raise or lift. Also *s'élever*: to lift oneself or rise in rank

The term commonly translated as 'to rise' is not the same as 'to stretch', although it may appear so to the dancer rising through the feet to *demi-pointe* and finally *sur les pointes*. Even in the earliest exercises the dancer should feel that he is raising the weight of the body into the air away from the floor, particularly the upper torso away from the pelvis at the waistline, and is not merely stretching or spreading to ease tension. This feeling of raising the weight of the body into the air is extremely important. It is intimately connected with correct breathing and with any *grand rond de jambe* where the torso is lifted very slightly upwards from the supporting leg as the working leg moves from side to back and in reverse. It is also intimately connected with movements such as *grands jetés en tournant*, *grands fouettés sautés* and rotation, when a dancer has to move swiftly into an *arabesque* during a turn.

It is not, however, only the torso that has to be raised. The leg has to be raised into a *battement relevé*. Whereas in a *développé* the leg is bent as it is raised, employing

To rise and raise

To jump (*grand jeté élancé*)

certain muscles to lift half the weight and to hold the leg at the correct height while other muscles stretch the leg outwards, in a *battement relevé* the full weight and length of the leg have to be lifted and controlled at an angle away from the body and the leg stretched at the same time. The arms, too, can be lifted to various heights and at different angles. It is important always to remember that both arms and legs are raised from underneath and once in position are held by muscles lying over the limb in question.

The act of raising and adjusting the head when the dancer stretches out of or into a bend can mean the difference between recovering or losing balance.

---

4   *Sauter:* to jump, leap or skip

5   *Elancer:* to push with strength. *S'élancer:* to dart

6   *Glisser:* to step, slide or glide. *Chasser:* to chase, hunt, drive out or break cover

---

If the definitions of these verbs are studied carefully in relation to dance, the dancer will see that the movements are very different although each one entails some degree of spring from the feet in order to travel.

Any kind of jump, leap or skip (*saut*) requires the strongest possible push away from the floor so that the body, whether moving upwards *en place* or travelling in no matter which direction, must be seen to soar away from the floor and to be held momentarily at the height of the jump. The impetus required to propel it upwards varies a great deal and must be properly understood if the line is to be correctly drawn.

Any *élancé* movement should find the dancer making a strong push away from but only just over the floor. This type of movement should never travel upwards. The difference between an *élancé* and a *sauté* movement is nowhere better exemplified than when dancing a *pas de basque élancé*, where the dancer seems to dart over the surface like a bird, and a *grand saut de basque*, where he must soar upwards, opening the leg outwards and/or making a turn at the height of the jump (see page 69).

To glide

A *glissé* movement also contrasts with a *sauté* or an *élancé* step. It has nothing of the same exhilaration or strength. The dancer must appear to be gliding on and along the surface so that the tips of the toes scarcely leave the floor. There is no upward movement as in *sauté*, nor any powerful push onwards as in an *élancé* step; nor, in purely classical ballets, should there be any of the sliding or slipping which is legitimate in such *demi-caractère* ballets as *Les Patineurs* where the dancers must appear to glide on ice.

Some dancers seem to believe that *glissades* and other *glissé* movements do not require much thought. They should remember that the *glissade* is one of the most valuable preparations for many kinds of jump. Every care should be taken to see, firstly, that it is carrying the dancer onwards in the appropriate direction from the moment it begins; secondly, that it is completed at the exact point in the flow of line when the jump or other movement must commence; and, thirdly, that it gives the correct impetus to what will follow. To ensure that this will happen, the dancer must co-ordinate all the movements of his head and arms with the step and with the music (see page 50).

A *chassé* is another step which carries the dancer onwards on the surface. The last meaning, 'to drive out', is the most appropriate for it defines a step which was originally (Feuillet 1702) a single movement from a 5th position *demi-plié* into 4th position *demi-plié*, the sole of the foot keeping full contact with the floor and the legs not being stretched. It is frequently used as a firm preparation for a *pirouette* or pose. The pressure of the sole of the foot along the floor throughout gives the impetus for the rise into the turn or pose. It is unlike any *pas glissé* done at speed when only the tips of the toes keep contact with the floor.

7   *Tourner*: to turn, or revolve

Weaver (1723) was the first to describe the dancer's ability to turn the leg outwards from the hip because of the nature of the ball and socket joint. He noted that a similar action took place in the arm socket and that some rotation could also be made at the wrist, knee and ankle. In describing the limited rotation at these three places he was careful to add how important it was that no rotation took place at the ankle: in classical dance, as he knew it and as it is today, if any rotation occurs at the ankle there is little likelihood of the dancer maintaining balance over the supporting leg. Weaver suggested, moreover, that only very careful rotation should be made at the knee because of the danger of displacement and of torn cartilages, although he allowed that such a 'flourish' added elegance to the line of the leg—just as today the *petits ronds de jambe en l'air* can add brilliance.

The turn of the hand at the wrist was all-important to Weaver because so much grace and courtesy lay in the play of the hand when holding or taking off the hat, when offered to a partner or during a bow—just as today's dancers must make that simple turn of the hand at the wrist every time they stretch their arms outwards into an *arabesque*. The dancer should make use of these limited movements of the hand at the wrist, because they give extra life and meaning to the line being followed in most *ports de bras*. They should always be simple and without fuss.

Such details tend to be forgotten because a study of turning has come to mean how to increase the number of *pirouettes* or *tours en l'air* that a dancer can perform in succession. Yet it is only when the dancer has mastered the swift, accurate turn of the head as he spins round, his eyes controlled to focus on the point at which the *pirouette* or *tour* is to end, that he can turn with confidence. The turn of the head must be co-ordinated with the impetus given by the supporting leg, the breath and the proper use of the arms. It is only when the pieces are pulled together—so to speak—that the dancer can hope to attain that degree of speed and excitement which Petipa felt *pirouettes* added to the dance (see page 79).

The co-ordination of all parts of the body can be achieved only by constant practice of the rules that derive from the first six principles already discussed and their application to the particular movement being performed.

There are seven types of movement in Petipa's vocabulary (described in the next section of this book). They are, of course, never danced in isolation and they have to be co-ordinated into *enchaînements* and ultimately into complete dances. These are arranged by the teacher or choreographer to suit the purpose of an exercise or the content of a ballet.

To turn (*tour en l'air*)

The Petipa Vocabulary

When studying Petipa's own notes for his many ballets and discussing these with the Soviet critic Yuri Slonimsky, it became clear that Petipa had made his own vocabulary and used each category of step in a particular way to give style and quality to each dance he created and bequeathed a repertoire of solos and *pas de deux* which are still used to test dancers' technical abilities throughout the world of classical ballet.

His ballets were mainly for French and Italian ballerinas whose technique was extremely polished. Although he demanded perfection of every step within an *enchaînement*, he was always careful to give each step only as much value as he felt necessary to make it play its proper part in the flow of line. It should, therefore, be clearly understood that the steps which Petipa referred to as preparatory play an absolutely major role in some dances. For this reason they must always be performed as accurately as possible and with their appropriate value, e.g. the purely classical walk or *pas marchés* of the *danseur noble* in any of the great *pas de deux* of *The Sleeping Beauty* or *Swan Lake*.

The Preparatory Steps

'To be a preparation or provide a link between one movement and the next.' (Petipa Archives)

The study of the preparatory steps must always begin with the bend and stretch-out of a *demi-plié* during which the dancer decides how much depth and strength are required to give impetus to the following movement (see page 29 rule 2). In addition, the timing of a *demi-plié* is all important. A slow, very controlled *demi-plié* may be excellent if, for example, the dancer is to step into a pose during an *adage*. However, such timing could wreck a jump of *grande élévation* or a multiple *pirouette*, both of which might be better with a swift and all-but-imperceptible quarter *plié*. The context and line of every *enchaînement* can vary so considerably that each has to be taken separately.

It is impossible to lay down absolutely firm rules about the timing of any *demi-plié*. Each dancer ultimately decides the appropriate timing and control to suit his own physique and technique. Moreover, a dancer will always remember to adjust his own timing to suit the choreographic plan and music so that timing plays its proper part no matter how far it may deviate from the normal class-room practice.

It is the same with every preparatory step, because not only must it give the necessary impetus but it must also be adapted to the time signature and speed of the *enchaînement*. The alterations that can take place in any step are quickly understood if it is first danced, for example, to a simple 2/4 beat and then to a 3/4, 4/4, 6/8 or even 5/8. This exercise soon reveals how the quality of a step changes if a musical flow of line is to be maintained. It is particularly interesting in such steps as *pas de bourrée* or *pas de basque* which require three beats if the three changes of weight are to have equal value. When they are danced to 2/4 one or other of the three steps has to be quickened or shortened, slowed or lengthened to keep within the two beats.

Such steps as the *pas de bourrée* and the *pas de basque* also change their quality according to the way they are performed. The former danced with almost straight legs can become smooth and elegant, particularly if turned *en dehors* or *en dedans* with a long stretch outwards and downwards at the beginning and a strong pull upwards during the turn. But if the dancer picks up each leg into a small *retiré* on every change of weight and dances more or less *en place* with or without turning, the step gains in speed and precision and—if *sur les pointes*—even brilliance. The *pas de basque* can absolutely change character. If it is *glissé*, it can be smooth and flowing; if *élancé* it has speed and darts like a bird over the surface, and can even be like a step of *grande élévation* ending in an exciting *attitude*. But the *pas de basque* can also be *sauté*, with the smallest or highest of jumps.

It is when practising such simple steps in the class-room that it is possible for the dancer to understand why so many conventional rules of the head and arms were formulated (see pages 27, 30). The old masters found that these helped to determine the direction to be taken and the impetus to be given to the following step. It is useful to add to these rules and to note that they apply principally to the moment when the preparatory step ends to take the dancer onwards into the next step and that they thus ensure the continuity of line.

1   For backward or sideways travel with the leading foot closing behind, the head should incline towards the supporting leg. But for travel forwards or sideways with the leading foot closing in front, the head should turn towards that foot. Both these points are particularly important when the dancer uses *épaulement* and when he moves into a large jump.

2   The arm on the same side as the leg closing in front should be bent across the body. But this will depend on what is to follow, because the arm may be needed to add impetus to some steps, e.g. when after a *glissade derrière* the dancer has to move into a *grand assemblé dessus*. In such a case, the bent arm must open in the same direction as the jump if the audience is to appreciate the height and length of the *assemblé*.

3   The arms, like the head, should move simply and economically in the direction of any jump or turn. Thus, in a *grand jeté en tournant*, the head should be erect and the arms in 5th position before the dancer turns in the air. Only during the turn will the head and body move into the *arabesque* line as the arms open into 2nd or into *arabesque*. Similarly in any *pirouette* with arms in 5th, the dancer will find that if the arms circle directly into 5th from 2nd and do not return to 1st before being lifted, not only will the turn gain speed but it will also look more spacious. This will also help the dancer to keep centrally balanced over the supporting leg.

It has already been emphasised that dancers must always be aware of the direction into which they are moving immediately the step begins (see page 19). They must also adjust the arms appropriately and exactly so that the total flow of line is achieved. The head can and should always anticipate that line independently.

Glissade écarté

Grand jeté en tournant

Petite et Grande Elévation

'To add lightness, depth and breadth to the dance.' (Petipa Archives)

The most important quality of any jump is the space it occupies combined with the direction it takes in the line of dance. The five jumps discussed earlier suggest their type and variety (see page 41). What also has to be understood is how to create the illusion of height (remembering that what goes up must also come down), length and breadth. Some jumps move only in one dimension once the dancer has stretched the legs out of a preparation. Others move through two or even three dimensions. The dancer must therefore demonstrate clearly the shape of the space being filled when a step of elevation is being performed. It is important when length is the dimension to be filled whether the total line is straight and narrow, e.g. a 'split' *jeté*, or straight and broad, e.g. *ailes de pigeon*; when rising or falling whether in a narrow or broad space, e.g. a *grand jeté en avant* or *grand jeté en tournant*. Alternatively, the total line may contain within it elements of various dimensions in some overall pattern which can follow a straight, diagonal, zig-zag, curved or—ultimately—a circular line.

Each jump has its conventional *ports de bras* which should be practised during the early stages of training. Time has proved that, for example, in any *échappé* such simple movements as the opening and raising of the arms from *bras bas* into a low *demi-bras* or 2nd position and then the lowering of them, when exactly co-ordinated with the legs opening from 5th to 2nd positions and back again, do help the dancer to gain height and thus keep the jump light. But the height of the jump will be increased if the dancer raises the arms from *bras bas* through 1st to 5th before lowering them to 2nd position as the legs descend into the open position.

The raising of the arms simultaneously with the jump upwards in order to lighten the weight of the body is vitally important in jumps such as *grand jeté entrelacé* and *en tournant*. For it is when the dancer has to project the line of a step into three dimensions, viz. height, length and breadth, that he must co-ordinate carefully every part of the body in order to fill the space convincingly and to stretch both arms and legs without over-complicating an already complex line, e.g. *grand jeté en tournant*, arms moving through 1st, 5th and into 2nd positions.

The second essential of any jump is the speed at which it is performed, for this can completely alter its quality. In most romantic ballets, notably *Giselle*, the heroine has to create the illusion that she is floating through the air, alighting for a moment and floating upwards again. To do so she must use the softest and most flowing of *grands jetés en avant* or *entrelacés* and *grands fouettés sautés*, practising them until she can get into the *arabesque* as she soars into the air, hold it at the height of the jump and still sustain it as she descends in a *fondu*. And she does this at a far slower tempo than the ballerina performing a 'flick' or 'split' *grand jeté* in a modern ballet, which above all requires speed if it is to have the athletic quality that it needs. The effect that the change of tempo can have on a step is most apparent in the *ports de bras*. In the slower tempo, arms appear softly rounded and are then stretched into a gentle *arabesque*, but at speed there is only time for one arm to be stretched after the other into a straight line and no time for the arms to pass through a rounded 1st position.

The action of the head is also different according to the tempo. As already noted, when drawing the romantic line, the head should already be stretched and curved with the back into the *arabesque* line as the jump begins and should then be sustained into the final pose. This pose must not be so set that it marks an end; it must be of such a nature that the dancer can proceed into the next step—something that all dancers in *Les Sylphides* must attempt if they are to go to, through and from the musical note as Fokine wished. The 'split' *jeté*, however, requires that the head be directed forwards into a straight line because the step's chief dimension is length; and the 'flick' *jeté* needs the head to be more upright in an *attitude* line as the dancer leaves the floor, and then to be directed backwards into an *arabesque* line as the leading foot is 'flicked' outwards.

Although these *jetés* require considerable strength, control and energy, the romantic style is more difficult to perform and co-ordinate with the music. Dancers who have good elevation frequently steal a little time by quickening their preparatory steps before the jump and thus spend longer in the air. This is particularly effective if they also land slowly and softly into an *arabesque fondue*. After that they can elongate their *arabesque* and ensure that the line they have followed can continue onwards into the next step or phrase. This continuous flow of line is the vital essence of such ballets as Fokine's *Les Sylphides* and Ashton's *Symphonic Variations*, two contrasted works which demonstrate clearly how in the hands of a great choreographer the class-room exercises acquire entirely different and new qualities.

Grande et Petite Batterie

'To add brilliance and sparkle, even wit.' (Petipa Archives)

Larousse: *Batterie:* the rough and tumble of a fight; musically, a quick succession of beats

---

It is difficult to understand why the term *batterie* was used in fourteenth-century horse-ballets to describe the swift beating of hooves round each other when the horses were reined up on their hind legs to perform a *cabriole*. The later musical definition would have been more appropriate. However, both meanings derive from *battement*. This meant firstly 'the beat of drums', which even today accompanies soldiers as they quicken step, and secondly, and better for dancers, 'the fluttering of wings', which aptly describes the dancer's *brisés volés* in the famous Blue-Bird variation of *The Sleeping Beauty*.

Be that as it may, it is important to remember that the *petits battements sur le cou de pied* of the daily class are the basic movements of any step using *grande* or *petite batterie*.

'Flick' *jeté*

Nowhere is it more important and more difficult to achieve the 'hold' in the air than in *grande* and *petite batterie*, and nowhere is it more important to understand the dimensions into which the dancer is moving and the angle at which the body must be held in relationship to the angle of the legs to obtain the best results. Bournonville, following the examples of Vestris and Gardel, perfected his system of teaching *batterie* and set a standard for the The Royal Danish Ballet which few soloists in other schools have yet matched—although some Soviet and a few American and English soloists can emulate the same virtuosity when a choreographer gives them the opportunity. In modern classical ballets these opportunities are rare because in their efforts to increase the size of all jumps and the speed and numbers of *pirouettes* choreographers frequently forget to add the brilliance and sparkle that Petipa thought necessary.

The difficulty for the dancer of any beaten steps lies in having to rise into the air opening the leg or legs during the ascent, to begin the beat and close the legs at the height of the jump, then to open and close them again during the descent. This is comparatively easy when performing the first simple beats such as *entrechat quatre*, because there is only one opening and closing to change the feet at the height of the jump and a similar change before the descent. It is far more difficult to perform an *entrechat six* where there have to be three openings before the descent. Although the beat can be worked out in detail, i.e. one opening and close before the dancer reaches the height, one at the height of the jump and the third during the descent, this rarely happens unless practised slowly and persistently at the *barre*. Films of various dancers show that each of them has a different way of timing the beats and that each way is effective. Yet the most important feature of each performance shows that it is the strength of the jump upwards and the first emphatic opening of both legs which determines the clarity of the beat. What is particularly noticeable is the ease with which the legs open and close freely from the hip-joints to the toes. The weight of the body has been fully stretched away from the legs and is correctly centred whether the legs are fully stretched (Russian style) or slightly bent (Italian style) during the jump.

Needless to say, all kinds of *changements, royales* and *entrechats* are, in essence, easier to perform because they are danced *en place* and from two feet to two feet so that the body has to be propelled upwards only. Provided that the dancer remembers the rules given earlier (see page 41) he can concentrate on the timing of the opening and closing of the legs. However, as soon as the beaten step has to travel in any direction and/or dimension, then the body has to be adjusted not only to the direction in which the legs will travel but also to the angle at which they are lifted. For the most part it is usual to follow the rules given for the five jumps. When the dancer has swiftly to adjust the body during a series of steps with few or no steps between the beats, he must use a slight tilt of the pelvis forwards and up again and co-ordinate this with a slight curve of the upper torso forwards, and backwards into the *arabesque* line.

The slight movement of the body to and fro with the beating of the feet forwards and backwards is best seen in the *brisés volés* of the Blue Bird in *The Sleeping Beauty*. If the dancer is to convey the impression of a bird fluttering as it flies through the air, then he must rise as high as he can and stretch slightly forwards over his legs as they beat *en avant* while he stretches both arms outwards and sideways at different levels. He must then reverse the movement, sweeping and beating the legs to the back and curving his body slightly backwards as he reverses his arms. He can give the impression of flying only if his arms move freely and simply up and down in their sockets leaving the shoulders calm and more or less level as the body moves to and fro and draws the appropriate line. The body must be fully centred at that brief moment when the legs pass each other through 1st position in the air. It is in steps like this that the phrasing of the music can be of the greatest help. Correctly done, the beat of the feet should coincide with the beat of the music. This helps the dancer to inhale and to hold the breath momentarily as he jumps and beats.

A *brisé* in its earliest and simplest form was little more than the working leg, with knee bent and toes pointed, brushing and beating at the back—and then at the front—of the supporting leg before the dancer stepped onwards on that foot (i.e. *petit battement* into a *pas marché*). It is possibly for this reason that in the Russian school the dancer begins from 5th or 4th position with the Right foot behind, brushes it forwards with a spring from the Left which beats behind and in front of the Right whilst in the air, and lands on the Right foot just before the Left descends into 5th. This *brisé* is also danced in reverse. Both versions are different from the *assemblé battu*, where the Right foot certainly brushes forwards but both feet beat equally and land simultaneously. Other schools begin, beat and finish *brisés* on both feet. These are more like the Russian *assemblés battus* and are generally more staccato in quality.

Whether the *brisés* are performed as *grande* or *petite batterie* the dancer should always use a very slight tilt of the pelvis and curve of the upper torso forwards or backwards in the direction travelled in order to get the best results. In this way the weight of the body is firmly centred over the legs at the moment of the spring upwards and as the legs are raised at an angle during the beat. The body then straightens as the feet land, or can be held at that very slight angle if other *brisés* are to follow. It is also valuable to use the law of alignment when performing *brisé devant* and that of *épaulement* when dancing *brisé derrière*.

Brisé volé devant (the beats and the finish)

Whereas in any *brisé* the body tilts to some degree in the direction travelled, in *cabrioles* the best results are obtained when the dancer's body inclines away from the direction and beat. The further a dancer is to travel in one direction and the higher the beat, the more important it is for the dancer to use his body to give the *cabriole* its proper place in the flow of line. This is difficult in any step based on a jump from one to the same foot. The movement of the body has to be very accurate so that at the height of the jump and beat it is part of the line which stretches and curves from the crown of the head to the tips of the toes. The arms can greatly help to achieve this line. But it must always be remembered that they only complement it. They should never be used so strongly that they throw the curve out of balance.

As in *brisés*, it is the subtle use of *épaulement* which can give extra qualities to the line drawn: for example, if in a *cabriole effacée devant* the arm on the same side as the supporting and thus springing leg is lifted into 5th position, then the body is slightly turned towards that arm to help the dancer curve the torso backwards more easily because the head is in front and can look under the arm—so to speak. In a *cabriole effacée derrière*, it is easier to stretch the arms into an *arabesque* line to complement the curve made by the legs and body during the jump and beat. It is also best to have in front the arm on the same side as the supporting-springing leg and to pay careful attention to the level at which it is held, so that the curve is seen to flow from the fingertips to the toes at the moment of the legs closing in the beat.

Cabriole derrière

Cabrioles à côté are rarely danced in classical ballet. They are essentially a peasant step widely used in Poland and Hungary. They are very difficult to dance with turned-out legs and soft ballet slippers as it is necessary to clip the heels together — without that movement they lose their essential quality. They do however appear occasionally in *demi-caractère* works such as *Dances at a Gathering* or in the *divertissements* of *Raymonda* and the finale of *The Sleeping Beauty*.

When such beats are added to such steps as *grands jetés en tournant* or *grands fouettés sautés*, the dancer must take into account the rules given for the five jumps (see page 41) and endeavour to rise and 'hold' in the air slightly longer. To do this he must give greater impetus to the preparation, timing it carefully so that it helps him to rise more slowly and beat with the musical phrasing and tempo.

Ports de Bras

'To lend continuity to the flow of line, help to give impetus to the movement and complete the total pattern of the steps.' (Petipa Archives)

It has already been noted that the arms convey style as they frame the body and head, playing a vital part in conveying expression and meaning. The dancer must therefore use them with sensitivity, co-ordinating their movement with the rhythm, tempo and quality of the musical phrasing, because the musical phrasing indicates the line to be translated into dance terms. To be legato, smooth-flowing and circling onwards through one *épaulement* or alignment to another without ceasing, *ports de bras* may nevertheless be exact in timing. The dancer must know that the position reached on a certain beat is exact, but it is not held even momentarily as it is only part of a continuing line. Or *ports de bras* may be more staccato, each position being held momentarily on the beat, and then taken directly onwards to another position on the next beat. Or the arms may be held still through many steps which culminate in a fine pose, demanding a complicated *port de bras* and a change of *épaulement* involving the dancer in a complete change of direction.

Variations on the above theme are endless. But no matter how much the arms may be changed, the dancers must, above all, keep the upper half of the body absolutely under control yet flexible if the arms are to convey that calm, gracious dignity essential to classical dance. (O.E.D. Aplomb: perpendicularity; self-possession. O.E.D. Self-possession: cool; composed; composure in agitating circumstances.) No matter how fast, how difficult, how involved the changes to be made in the line of dance, the dance must behave as the Russians say: 'As if your shoes belong. Come on to the stage as if you own it! It is yours, therefore give yourself to the dance, not to the problems of technique.'

One way of achieving aplomb is for the dancer to move the arms in lines parallel to those drawn by the feet. For example: in a simple *glissade* the arms begin in 3rd position with the feet in 5th, open into 2nd as one foot moves outwards, and one of

Romantic *port de bras*

Modern *port de bras*

them closes in 3rd as the feet close again. Or: in a *pas de basque en avant*, the arms begin as in a *glissade*, the same arm and leg circle outwards to 2nd and then, as the weight is transferred forwards through 1st to 4th position, both arms circle to *bras bas* and 1st before opening again to 2nd or 3rd as the feet close. The dancer thus fills his sphere with a circular movement and creates a horizontal dance pattern. As an alternative, the dancer may circle the leading arm up to 5th before lowering it through 2nd, *bras bas* and 3rd during the whole *pas de basque*. In this case, the sphere is filled with both horizontal and vertical patterns.

An essential function of any *port de bras* is to help the dancer to maintain balance. It is therefore important to decide how the arms must be counterpoised at all times in order to keep the weight of the body centrally balanced. It is for this reason that the rules given earlier (see page 30) have come to be accepted as normal practice in the class-room. However, the arms can also be used as counterpoint to the movement of the feet. According to the Oxford English Dictionary, this term means 'a melody added as an accompaniment to a given melody'. This is certainly the interpretation made in many solos created by Petipa, where the dancer performs several steps with her legs whilst performing only one *port de bras*. Aurora does this in her solo following the Rose *Adage*, performing eight *petits jetés devant* whilst moving backwards BEFORE her arms circle from *bras bas* through 1st to 5th and down to 3rd position as a preparation for a swift *pirouette* and the final pose in *arabesque à terre*, arms also in *arabesque*. Both Fokine and Ashton use a great deal of counterpoint in their ballets, particularly in *Les Sylphides* and *Symphonic Variations*. It is this particularly calm, free-flowing style of *ports de bras* which allows the audience to appreciate the musical flow of line being created and, at the same time, the rhythmic beat and tempo of the footwork. Such co-ordination between all parts of the body marks the truly musical dancer.

In the above ballets it is important to note that the arms are used both to counterpoise and counterpoint every *enchaînement* until not only is the dancer's personal sphere of movement filled, but also the stage. Only in this way can the various steps and *ports de bras* in co-ordination and co-operation travel through all the possible dimensions of height, depth, length and breadth of the dance and its music.

Pirouettes

'To add speed and excitement.' (Petipa Archives)

Like the words *cabriole, chassé, déboulé* and others, *pirouette* seems to have derived from a term used in hunting and horse-riding. By the mid-fifteenth century (1450) the word 'pirouelle' had been changed to *pirouette*, a term used when a horse made a turn without changing ground. All the above terms can be found in descriptions of

Arabesque en tournant

fourteenth and fifteenth century horse-ballets staged by French and Italian kings and prelates. The term 'pirouelle' would seem to have originated in the Italian 'pirole' or Norman 'Piroue' (diminutive 'pirouette'), both meaning a top. Another source could have been the Franco-Norman-Guernsey word 'piroue' meaning a little wheel or a whirligig, a child's toy. The second derivation could have given rise to a French critic's stern condemnation of Auguste Vestris, the self-styled god of the dance: 'He turns and turns flailing his arms round like a windmill.' No doubt this was prejudiced criticism. Or was it because Vestris was dancing in a *demi-caractère* ballet? In such ballets a dancer may and does whip the arms up and down: in *Les Patineurs* one Blue Girl does this as she whirls round the stage with great speed and effect. In older classical ballets such movements would be frowned upon because the dancers would be unable to keep cool, calm and collected when expending energy so extravagantly. Nor could the Blue Boy retain his aplomb as he spins round with his body almost horizontal to the stage in a series of *grands jetés en tournant*.

Nevertheless, *pirouettes* in classical ballets must not lack speed or excitement if they are to arouse interest in the dance. In fact, it is the sudden turn of speed which can become the high-point of an *enchaînement* even in such a *pas de deux* as that of Act II of *Swan Lake* where, in the middle of a passage after a slow preparation, Odette suddenly expresses her feelings with a multiple *pirouette*, stops face to face with Siegfried and as suddenly bends backwards away from him as if afraid to let him see how much she has fallen in love. This *pirouette* has a very different quality and purpose than the famous thirty-two *pirouettes fouettées* in Act III which Odile dances very deliberately to dazzle Siegfried so that he forgets the lyrical Odette's unexpected expression of love.

The above examples are only two of many where *pirouettes* or *tours* are used to give greater emotional content to the dance. It is equally important to understand how the *pirouette* (or *tour*) should be performed when it is not the high-point of an *enchaînement* or dance, but only one of a series leading to some gesture or pose—as in the Rose *Adage*, when Aurora's gesture of taking a rose from one of her Suitors is far more important than the *pirouette* which precedes it. She has to perform this gesture four times because she has four Suitors. As she favours no one more than another, she has to give exactly the same impetus and use exactly the same timing as she turns with each one of them. This requires very strict discipline for it is well known that as a dancer repeats an *enchaînement* containing *pirouettes* it usually becomes easier and more exciting to perform—something that happens in the final *pas de deux* of *The Sleeping Beauty* where, again, the sequence is repeated four times. But this time Aurora increases the number of *pirouettes* before being held in the final triumphant pose, Queen of her whole court.

These examples demonstrate the importance of timing for a *pirouette*. The first example (Odette) expresses a surge of emotion and must be fast if it is to make its effect. The second (Odile) is meant as a virtuoso trick to bedazzle Siegfried and also the audience. The third (Aurora for her Suitors) is a preparation for a gesture, and if too fast and brilliant the meaning of the gesture is lost. The final example (Aurora with the Prince) marks the triumph of the ballerina as Princess, completely awake and in command of her stage, her kingdom of classical dance.

The last example also demonstrates how important it is for the dancer to be able to increase the number of turns from a simple preparation but with no increase in the tempo of the music. It is this ability to increase the number of turns within the tempo set that requires the greatest control over impetus and timing. Each dancer must know exactly how much impetus to give to the arm coming into the turn, as well as to the rise from the *demi-plié*, to the breath and to the action of the head. Each dancer should also be in control over his weight and keep it centred over the supporting leg so that he is able to finish the *pirouette* firmly by lowering the supporting heel exactly at that moment and at that point in the personal sphere which will ensure that the final pose or position is held. It is the holding of the final pose or position which is so important to the onlooker. Without it the *pirouette* lacks finish because the dancer has lost his aplomb and sense of line.

When performing any *pirouette* the dancer must remember to centre the weight fully over whichever leg will be supporting when moving out of the preparation. It is on these occasions that the dancer must understand and use the length of his leg fully, and take the preparatory position in such a way that the rise to *demi-* or full *pointe* only requires a strong stretch upwards of the supporting leg (see page 29). It should never be necessary to push the body forwards at the same time as foot and leg stretch upwards, except on occasions where the dancer turns in *arabesque*. This *pirouette* is usually taken *en dedans* from 4th position. The dancer should take care that the body is fully centred over the front leg *fondue* with the upper back held firmly, but already stretched slightly backwards so that he moves directly into the *arabesque* line as the working leg pushes upwards from the floor with the stretch out of the preparation into the *relevé* and *pirouette*.

This same placing of the weight directly over the supporting leg is equally important in all *pirouettes posées* whether moving *en dehors* or *en dedans* and most particularly when the dancer is moving *sur les pointes* round the stage. The moment she steps on to her *pointe*, her body must be directly over that leg, its weight centrally balanced. This centring of weight on every turn is vital if the *manège* is to be exact, for it is only when the weight is correctly centred that the head will be able to work freely and the eyes adjust themselves to find the new point to which the dancer must direct her next step.

Tours en l'air

It is generally accepted that the term *pirouette* means any kind of step when the dancer turns on one leg only. A *tour* is generally accepted to mean a step where the dancer turns equally on one after the other foot, as in *pirouettes enchaînées* or in *emboîtés*, or jumps and turns in the air off both feet. When performing any of the latter, the dancer needs to study the rules given for the five jumps and use them appropriately. The principal difficulty of such turns is the absolute need to co-ordinate the impetus given by the shoulder moving into the turn with the jump away from the floor. This action of the arm has already been discussed in the description of *grands jetés en tournant* and *grands fouettés sautés* which are comparatively simple half turns and can be practised at the *barre* so that the rise and fall of the body into the *arabesque* can be controlled (see page 41). But once a full turn has to be made during any kind of jump the dancer must decide how much impetus is required from both the shoulder coming into the turn and from the leading arm which must be co-ordinated with the jump from the floor.

Simple *tours en l'air*, jumping from two feet to two feet, are the first to be mastered because they set the pattern for all other *tours*. The first essential is to understand that at the moment of sinking into the preparatory *demi-plié*, the hips and shoulders must be level and parallel to each other, exactly facing that particular point in the personal sphere at which the tour will begin and end, at least in the early stages. The second essential is that, during the pressure downwards with arms in 3rd position, the weight must remain centrally balanced over the two feet and remain there as the dancer springs upwards just after opening the leading arm into 2nd and then brings both arms into a shortened 1st position. When making this swift movement of the arms, the dancer must be very careful not to twist the shoulder coming into the turn to give extra impetus, nor must he incline the head in any way. The head must turn only from side to side as the eyes focus and re-focus on the point where the step is to end. Once in the air the dancer must hold the position gained on leaving the floor and make no further movement until the tips of the toes reach the floor. Only then should the fully stretched legs begin to bend as the weight of the body descends.

The need to keep the hips and shoulders level and directed to one point of the personal sphere is of vital importance during the preparation for all other types of *tours en l'air*. It is also of great importance to decide exactly at what level and angle the body, head, leg or legs have to be held during the turn. For example, in a *grand saut de basque en tournant* is the vital throw of the leg upwards to be into 4th position *devant*, or *écarté*? If it is to be in front, then the dancer should be seen to direct his leg to that point and to complete his *tour en l'air* with the other leg in *retiré* at the same point at which the turn began. If, on the other hand, the throw is into *écarté* (or *à la seconde* at 90°), then the dancer should finish in *écarté*. The throw in front is best when the dancer is travelling in a diagonal, but the throw to *écarté* is best when circling round the stage. The exact placing of the body is even more important if the dancer is attempting a double or triple *tour* as he jumps. He must always soar into the air from one or both feet and must already be turning at the height of the jump. He must also be very careful not to displace the central axis round which he is apparently turning by throwing his arms widely apart or behind his shoulders as he rises; rather he should draw them into a shortened 1st or raise them directly into 5th position as clearly and swiftly as possible.

The firm control over the placing of the body and legs in the correct direction and alignment to be held during a *pirouette* or *tour* is even more important during any form of supported *adage* and lifts where the girl must maintain her centre line of balance throughout the turn or turns, particularly if she is thrown upwards into the air from her partner's arms to do a double or triple *tour* before being caught again in the position in which she began turning, and before she is lowered into another pose. An excellent example of this 'hold' before a drop is in Aurora's final *pas de deux* with her Prince where she performs *pirouettes en dedans* from a low *arabesque* after placing both hands on his outstretched arm as a preparation and then falls into the 'fish'. She must complete her *pirouette* with her spine erect and, only as she falls and feels her partner's arm catch her body, must she stretch her head and upper back into the *arabesque* line and bend her erstwhile supporting-turning leg upwards at the knee. A somewhat similar throw upwards into the air as mentioned above is also performed thus: the girl being thrown upwards and turned before being dropped into a horizontal position parallel to the floor. In both examples she must keep the whole of her body fully stretched from the crown of her head to the tips of her toes throughout the *tour*, in the same way that the boy must do in his triple *tours en l'air*.

Pirouettes enchaînées

Larousse: *Enchaîner*: to link

The exact placing of the body in relationship to the direction to be travelled will determine the success or otherwise of those turning movements which are called variously *pirouettes enchaînées* or *petits tours*. These quick spins are usually taken diagonally across the stage and although differently named are nearly identical in performance, being a series of quick turns on one then on the other foot to make one complete *tour*. As the term *enchaîné* means linked, it would seem that in the old French school *pirouettes enchaînées* were performed with the feet moving in 5th position. In other words, the dancer starts *pointe tendue devant*, head in the *écarté* line, then steps forward into the line of dance making a half turn, circles the other foot to 5th *devant*, and completes the other half turn on that foot as if performing a *détourné* so that it finishes in 5th position *derrière*. The dancer is thus able to step outwards again. This particular way of turning is most effective for the girl dancing *sur les pointes* for she cannot step too far outwards with a large step which would spoil the daintiness and speed of the movement. She should use the most delicate of *ports de bras*, not opening the leading arm too far into 2nd as she steps on to the front foot, and swiftly closing both arms into a shortened 1st as the feet close together in 5th position.

Déboulés

Larousse: *Débouler*: to roll or fall from the top to the bottom

---

As the above definition suggests, the term *déboulé* best describes the extremely fast *pirouettes enchaînées* usually performed by the male dancer in sheer exuberance at the end of a virtuoso solo. He dances them on three-quarter or *demi-pointes* and starts as before from *pointe tendue devant* towards the audience, stepping into *écarté* to make a half turn. He thus finishes more or less back to the audience whilst circling the other foot forwards into 1st, and spins on to complete the other half turn facing the audience again. As for the girl closing in 5th, the step must be small and the legs must be kept fully stretched, the weight of the body fully centred throughout the movement. It is usual for the boy to give impetus from the shoulder coming into the turn on the first movement only, for once he has started to spin the sheer speed of his footwork and proper use of his head should carry him onwards.

In both *pirouettes enchaînées* and *déboulés* the head is of vital importance if speed is to be gained and maintained. If the dancer starts *écarté* to the line of dance, his head is already turned towards the point at which the first half turn should finish. Then all he or she has to do is to turn it swiftly and re-focus that point to complete the other half turn.

Emboîtés

Larousse: *Emboîter:* to place one thing inside another

The simplest form of *emboîté* is performed by the girl when, beginning from 5th position *sur les pointes*, she lowers her heels and, with a slight *fondu* or sometimes none at all, she stretches the back foot out sideways and brings it quickly back to 5th position *devant* and immediately repeats the movement with the other foot. She must follow the rules of *épaulement* and slightly change her shoulder-line with each step, bringing forward the shoulder on the same side as the foot that is coming in front, and at the same time very slightly turning her head towards that foot. Performed at speed the step requires that the dancer actually put one foot into the other's place, hence the term *emboîté*.

But the more usual form of *emboîté* is that where the dancer springs from one foot to the other, making a half turn with each *petit jeté*, and uses a head movement similar to that used in *pirouettes enchaînées*. These turns are very difficult to keep neat when the dancer is travelling across the stage because there is often too much effort made to travel on the first of the *petits jetés* leaving the second to be performed *en place*. But if the dancer will remember the rule given earlier for *petits jetés* (see page 46) and adjust the alignment very carefully during the spring upwards, it will be found that although the preparation is the same as for *pirouettes enchaînées* and *déboulés*, the first *jeté* must find the dancer springing upwards and forwards making a clear half turn in the air before landing, and then making another clear half turn with the second *jeté* to complete the movement. Only by making these clear half turns in the air can the dancer whip the jumping leg outwards to travel and then bring it back under the body—allowing the other leg to whip out equally far and to help the dancer to make the next half turn that completes the movement.

The *port de bras* for such turns is usually a simple but small opening of the arms alternately into 2nd position and back again into a shortened 1st, simultaneously with the opening and closing of the legs. As the arm on the same side as the leg is working, the dancer should realise that there is a slight change of *épaulement* with each *jeté*. The faster the movement, the smaller should be the *ports de bras* and the

Arabesque penchée

quicker and more accurate the action of the head and eyes to focus on the direction travelled.

Poses (*Arabesques, attitudes, etc.*)

'To become the high-light or finishing point of an *enchaînement* or dance.' (Petipa Archives)

O.E.D. Pose: assume an attitude especially for artistic purposes; attitude of body or mind, especially one assumed for effect

Both definitions of the term 'pose' are particularly apt when applied to classical ballet. In most of Petipa's choreography a pose is usually struck and held in order to allow the audience to admire the prowess of the performer, who maintains aplomb no matter how difficult the preparation for the pose and its resolution. However, Fokine, in his more classical ballets, hoped his dancers would feel that the poses were only part of a continuing line and not an item of particular value. He wrote: 'The *arabesque* [in *Les Sylphides*] is a very apparent gesture. It is a yearning for height, distance, an inclination of the body, a movement of the entire being. It is there instead of words.' Yet even though the differences between *arabesques* may seem very evident, they only appear so if the dancer distinguishes between Petipa's purely classical style of technique and Fokine's 'romantic reverie'.

Much of this difference in style can be explained by the different approaches these two great choreographers made to their music. For Petipa it was a time-keeper, as can be understood by a study of the orders which he sent to Tchaikovsky for the score of *The Sleeping Beauty*. He gave the composer the time-signatures, tempos, number of bars, sometimes even the instruments he preferred, as well as brief descriptions of what the music was supposed to represent. Petipa is even known to have returned parts of scores which he had commissioned from Minkus and Pugni, those composers of 'Special Ballet Music', because they did not conform to the standard dances that he expected, such as waltzes, polkas, gallops, etc.

Fokine, on the other hand, tried in *Les Sylphides* and other ballets to interpret the music chosen and to give visual form to the melody, rhythm, tempo and phrasing. It is this visual interpretation of music by dance that is the vital feature of certain ballets by Ashton, Balanchine, Robbins and others. Their methods and styles vary considerably but in each of their works can be found *enchaînements* which parallel the rise and fall of the melody, its rhythms and phrasings, its diminuendos and accelerandos, its pianissimos and fortissimos—indeed the whole range of directions given by a composer to the musicians. This is why today's classical dancers must pay greater attention to the musical details. No longer do choreographers, as Petipa did, repeat an *enchaînement* four times just because the earlier composers of Special Ballet Music usually repeated their phrases four times (conforming to the rules laid down by Lully and Rameau, composers of the King's Dance Music, i.e. suites of court dances). Today, choreographers interpreting the music of Bach, Beethoven and Brahms, or modern masters such as César Franck, Shostakovitch, Stravinsky and Britten, frequently find themselves creating long *enchaînements* which do not repeat or, if they do, do so with many variations.

In such cases the dancers, too, have to pay much more attention to the comparative value of each step. It is in these long *enchaînements* that the various poses, properly timed, can help the audience to appreciate the flow of line because they act as do commas and semi-colons in a sentence. They draw attention to the dimensions of the pattern woven by the dancers as they move within their personal sphere over the stage. Today the pose is rarely an item in its own right, to be struck and held as part of a virtuoso feat such as Kitri's series of *relevés développés devant* at 90° across the stage in *Don Quixote*, where she performs two quick ones before holding the third for twice as long and repeats this series four times, holding the last pose for even longer—if the conductor allows this extravagance. Today, in most classical ballets, particularly those without a story or theme, the pose is only one step in a continuing line and takes on many different forms, so that it rarely looks like any practised in the class-room.

Arabesque

O.E.D. *Arabesque:* Arabian, fantastic

Until Blasis defined *arabesque* in terms of classical dance, the word was used, as it still is, to describe the curved decorations which catch the eye with their fantastic weavings on gateways, staircases and buildings in southern Spain. The beauty of the designs lies in the perfect balance of the curves, sometimes one within another no matter at what angle they are set. It is the shape of this perfectly balanced curve that the dancer has to create from the crown of the head to the tips of the toes of the working leg, and centre that curve directly over the supporting leg to create an *arabesque*. Once the curve has been achieved it can be tilted upwards or downwards, but it must never lose shape. This means that by changing the angle at which the *arabesque* is held, from its lowest *à terre* to the highest *arabesque penchée*, the choreographer and dancer have a marvellously varied pose to work into the flow of line. And this is not all that can change the look of an *arabesque*. The dancer can and often does stretch it into a slightly longer curve if he lands from a jump in a *fondu* before resuming the proper curve, because the spinal curves must be used as shock-absorbers if the landing is to be controlled and thus soft. As the dancer stretches upwards on the supporting leg, the same shock-absorbers react to stretch upwards again and the spine resumes the proper *arabesque* line, if it is to be held. The dancer may also perform the same stretch and elongate the curve if preparing to move backwards into a jump, which could send his body along a line all but parallel to the floor and then into a high *grand jeté élancé*, where an almost perpendicular *attitude* would be the high-point of the *enchaînement*.

In most *arabesques* the shoulders should be level and face a front, so the positions and uses of the arms are all important. These can only be exact if the dancer moves the arms freely within their sockets, particularly if one or both arms have to move behind the shoulders and body. This can be achieved only if the arm or arms are slightly lowered and turned in their sockets before they pass behind the shoulders and then travel backwards. It is a subtle movement, but is part of the continuous rounding and circling of the arms until the straightening of elbow and wrist when the limits of the *arabesque* have to be felt and seen. This final straightening is most difficult to achieve in those ballets, such as *Les Sylphides*, where the *arabesque* is only part of a continuing line. Fokine demanded that his *arabesques* go to, through and from the note because 'his dancers were lighter than air and must therefore never cease to appear as if hovering over, not on the ground.'

The syllabus of each classical dance school has numbered its own series of *arabesques*, which are distinguished one from the other by the way the arms are held in their relationship to the alignment and or *épaulement*. But in essence there are only two basic forms of *arabesque*: the dancer is either *effacé* or *croisé* to the audience as he curves the body and working leg, and sets that curve over the perpendicular supporting leg. There are countless variations, and not only in the level at which that curve can be tilted and the positions of the arms, but also in the placing of the body. The Russian fourth *arabesque* is only one example of how it can have an extra dimension if the upper back is curved and slightly twisted backwards towards the audience as the dancer poses *croisé*. There are other instances where the dancer's body can appear to relax so far forwards that he all but falls, only slowly to recover and, if a girl, to rise *sur les pointes*—and softly and smoothly to float across the stage with *pas de bourrée suivis*, as she does in *Giselle*.

Attitude

O.E.D. Attitude: posture of body; disposition of figure

In 1820, Blasis quoted the statue of the Flying Mercury by Giovanni da Bologna as the ideal *attitude* for classical dancers to study. Before his time, the term 'attitude' had been used to describe any pose taken by the dancer—in any position whether the working leg was *à terre* or *en l'air*, either in front or at the back, bent or straight.

The important thing about the Mercury is that the sculptor represented the messenger of the gods in flight. Wings are on his helmet and ankles to indicate his swift movement. His body is inclined at an angle to denote speed—for is he not also the god of all travellers and of animals? He holds a wand in his lower hand, with the other arm raised forwards and upwards, seemingly towards the heavens for his eyes

Mercury

Classical *attitude*

gaze upwards at the beckoning finger. He displays the law of opposition and curves his body towards the supporting leg. Otherwise he would surely fall to earth for he moves as if propelled onwards by a puff of wind. This statue is equally rewarding no matter at which angle it is examined. Yet the pose is seldom performed in this way today, presumably because the legs are not turned out and the whole position may appear too unconventional to the average classical dancer. Nevertheless, every dancer should study the placing of the limbs of the statue because the whole is a marvellous example of how to counterbalance the arms and legs in order to maintain equilibrium.

Blasis himself was a fine draughtsman. A glance at his sketches of the varying *ports de bras* which he used for *attitudes* reveals how well he placed each particular pose at the best angle from the audience's point of view. Thus, if the dancer is *de face* or *croisé derrière* to the audience, then the upper part of the raised leg is directly bent behind the body, the lower leg being bent as far as possible at a right-angle so that it can be seen at all times. If, however, the dancer is standing *effacé*, the raised leg is not held at such an acute angle so that the audience can still see the line of the whole leg, although it is bent away from them. Another interesting thing to note when studying Blasis's sketches is the important part played in the total picture by the well-opened yet slightly tilted shoulders to give the impression that the dancer is really moving and is not frozen into a pose. It should be added that Blasis wrote: 'All poses of the body should be *épaulé*, especially the head, otherwise the effect will be lifeless.'

Blasis's sketches of other *attitudes, arabesques* and poses make it evident that dancers from his school were able considerably to change the look of any pose by altering the height of the leg, by slightly changing the line of the shoulders and the *épaulement*, or by the placing of arms and head, even though the height to which the leg was raised was nothing like the same as it is today. The change in the height of the leg in any pose whatsoever took place and increased as dancers discarded tunics, knickers and shirts, and instead wore tights and leotards for practice, which do not impede movement. Moreover, since technique has developed and extensions of the leg have become greater and higher, dancers have found that proper development of a 'muscular corset' has strengthened their spines and allowed them to maintain aplomb without in any way impeding their movements. Rather the 'corset' increases the need for mobility from the waist upwards and from the hip-joints downwards because the spinal curves have to be used continuously and carefully as shock-absorbers for the high leaps, multiple turns, *pirouettes* and *enchaînements* of great difficulty that today's choreographers and audiences expect. If the spine does not respond and become part of the flow of line, part of the total movement is lost and the dancers usually injure themselves whilst failing to follow the pattern laid down.

Grands Poses Devant, à la Seconde and Ecartés

Larousse: *Ecarter*: to throw wide open

There are only three *grands poses* to be considered. These demand that the working leg be stretched outwards and forwards, sideways, or at an angle to the side, i.e. *écarté* at 90° or above. As with the *arabesque* so much will depend on the context of the *enchaînement* or dance in which they appear. In each case, the dancer may step from one pose into another or can fall towards the raised leg in a small, normal or large position in order to extend the flow of movement. The size of position will depend on what is to follow. If only a small position is needed, perhaps to be used as a preparation for a *pirouette en dehors*, then all that is required is to drop the raised leg straight downwards and to transfer weight over both feet just after the sole of the raised foot reaches the floor. If a larger (normal) position is needed, then the dancer falls towards the raised leg just after it begins to fall. But for the largest position, the dancer must rise on *demi-* or full *pointe*, leaning slightly away from the raised leg, and then gradually fall towards it, trying to keep the legs as far apart as possible and only allowing the body to curve towards the point at which the raised leg will ultimately descend just as its toe reaches the ground. Such a fall requires the greatest control over legs and body and, as has already been stated, the dancer must move directly towards the point at which he is travelling and in the exact *épaulement* or alignment the moment the movement begins.

Both *grands poses à la seconde* and *écartés* can also be performed by the dancer moving away from the raised leg. In the first case it is usual to bend (in a *fondu*) the supporting leg and to lean slightly away from the raised leg before lowering it to the ground close behind the supporting leg and moving, for example, in a *pas de bourrée*. The movement of falling towards or away from the raised leg is even more effective when performed *écarté*, that is, when the dancer is at an angle to the front of the stage and is moving along a diagonal line. It is the angle of the head turned directly over one shoulder and in front of the raised arm in an *écarté devant*, or towards and looking away from the raised leg and arm in an *écarté derrière*, which seems to make the line drawn more emphatic. This is particularly so if the dancer has to change *épaulement* during the fall and does this towards the audience. It happens when he takes *développé écarté devant* and falls into an *arabesque épaulée*. In other words, having thrown the body and leg into a wide open position, the dancer falls and, during the fall, circles the raised arm backwards, the other forwards, as if to hide the body from view. This is a movement that occurs several times in Ashton's lyrical ballets, particularly when his dancer has to express shyness or withdrawal after being moved emotionally by the sheer joy expressed in dance.

It is when one comes to study Ashton's use of the various *grands posés*, particularly the *arabesques*, that one understands more than ever Fokine's words: 'An *arabesque* is a movement of the whole being, an expression, a belief in dance as a means of communication.' No matter which of Ashton's ballets one watches, there is an

Ecarté devant

Ecarté derrière

arabesque giving the dancers the means through which to communicate their feelings for the dance. The *arabesque* may be one part in the flow of line he has created or a very definite gesture to express some deep emotion. No dancer can fail to respond to his choreography, for there, within the movement, is all that can be said in dance. In place of words Ashton has created a vocabulary of unlimited meanings out of the principles and rules of the class-room technique. Such are his self-discipline and understanding of these unlimited meanings that each gesture and each movement fit the content of the particular ballet. The dancer is the medium through whom he speaks. The words are his, and for the audience they are like poems.

Pointes

'To add the finishing touch to the whole picture.' (Petipa Archives)

By the 1880s the French and Italian ballerinas employed by Petipa had mastered the new techniques first taught by Blasis and, with the help of the newly stiffened and blocked ballet shoes, were able to perform many virtuoso feats *sur les pointes*.

As in every other part in Petipa's vocabulary the dancer can use the *pointes* in many ways to differentiate and change the style and quality of the appropriate steps.

Before Petipa created his dances for *The Sleeping Beauty* (1890) he was aware of Bournonville's criticism that in his ballets: 'The dancers have run to technicalities and effects . . . all Petipa does is to create new difficulties for the dancers.' Not even 'the diabolical wind raised by their steel-like *pointes* and hearts of ice' could hold the interest of the Imperial St Petersburg audiences. It seemed that Petipa would have to go because the Treasury was losing money.

The Director, Vsevelozhsky, decided to give the choreographer one more chance and himself selected the subject he felt most suitable, worked out a skeleton plot and, before he approached Petipa, invited Tchaikovsky to compose the music. Needless to say, this annoyed Petipa who considered himself, and was so called by many in the Imperial Theatres, 'the Tsar's Director of the Imperial Ballet' and of all that went by way of dance at the Marinsky and at the Imperial Dancing Academy. Vsevelozhsky finally persuaded Petipa that he should put all his vast knowledge of the traditions of ballet at the services of the Marinsky in order to re-interest its audiences. The Director envisaged that *The Sleeping Beauty* would be set in the time of Louis XIV so that all the grace, elegance and refined tastes of that period could be displayed as a 'magnificence' on the Imperial stage. Surely, he felt, this must rekindle interest in an art that had all but degenerated into a series of endless *divertissements* which showed off the dancers' virtuoso tricks *sur les pointes*, and which employed complicated machinery and novel stage effects.

The Sleeping Beauty is still one of the greatest classical ballets and remains a testing ground for every ballerina because the five solos and three *pas de deux* give her a wonderful opportunity to display her mastery over Petipa's entire vocabulary of movement.

It is when watching these solos that one understands the subtle uses which Petipa so often makes of the *pointes*. There are some extremely difficult moments for Aurora during the long balances in *attitude* in the Rose *Adage* where she has to be in absolute control of herself and her technique. She requires an extremely strong foot, ankle and supporting leg, an ability to 'hold' her *attitude* without deviating in any way from the perpendicular even at those moments when she has to raise her hand upwards from one Suitor and then place it in the hand of the next. The *enchaînement* is even more demanding when it is repeated, for each Suitor, in turn, makes a promenade round Aurora as she 'holds' her *attitude*—until finally she has to make a supreme effort during the last few bars and stretch both legs and arms into a triumphant *arabesque*. Few realise the meticulous timing this feat requires from both Aurora and her Four Suitors in co-ordination with each other and the music. If this is achieved, then the audience can appreciate how one simple movement—a classical *attitude*—can become the high-point of a dance. No wonder they applaud, for the full flow of line within Aurora's personal sphere has been revealed and the fact that she stands *sur la pointe* lends the finishing touch to the whole picture.

A study of Aurora's solo in the last act reveals one very subtle movement when she steps delicately on to the front foot on *pointe* with the smallest *développé* and brings the back foot to it in a tight 5th, immediately opening the front foot again. When she begins she slightly leans forward as if watching her toe, but as she travels she gradually straightens her body and raises her arms from *demi-bras* to an open 5th position, making a tiny circling movement of her hands with each step (i.e. in Nijinska's version). In some way Aurora is beating out Tchaikovsky's rhythm, just as she makes the flow of his musical phrasing quite visible when she travels backwards and forwards with *pas de bourrée suivis*, pausing *sur la pointe* in one pose or another in her solo after the Rose *Adage*.

This marking of the beat, albeit silently, is performed by the three girls in Ashton's *Symphonic Variations* where they mark each beat in a series of *pas de bourrée sur les pointes* as one of the boys performs a solo which reveals the rise and fall of the melody and its phrasing. The whole passage is a remarkable example of counterpoint in classical dance.

Another interesting example of a dancer beating out the rhythm is found in Lise's solo at the picnic in *La Fille mal gardée* when she springs across the stage with the tiniest *petits jetés devant sur les pointes* travelled at great speed. This conveys a wonderful sense of joy and freedom. The dance follows shortly after Mother Simone's famous clog dance during which four of Lise's friends seek to emulate the old lady by dancing *sur les pointes* in their wooden sabots with the lightest of beats and the gayest of spirits. An example of how classical dancers can make the rhythm of a dance heard as well as seen by their footwork!

However, such a clatter of feet, no matter how delicate, is the very thing that dancers must avoid in ballets such as *Les Sylphides* and when dancing as Wilis in *Giselle*.

There is nothing so magical to a child than the ghost-like figure of the Queen of the Wilis who drifts silently across the stage at her first entrance. Softly she appears and disappears through the trees until finally she appears again, her beautiful yet cold face unveiled. Despite her silence and the lyrical quality of her *ports de bras*, her movement is purposeful, for her whole being assumes an air of command, an air she must retain until cock-crow when she, with the rest of the Wilis, must return to the grave.

There are countless examples of *pointes* being used to add the finishing touch to a movement or even to the interpretation of character. The perfect example is Ashton's stroke of genius in putting Bottom *sur les pointes* when he is changing into an Ass in *The Dream*. How else could a dancer convey the tiny yet sometimes clumsy hooves of that obstinate animal? It is also an example of how modern choreographers rarely use the *pointes* as pieces of machinery either to hold the dancer up during virtuoso feats or to make the dancer's legs look like machines at work as they did in the past.

Petipa did little for the male dancers at the Marinsky. He was uninterested in their distinctive male style and type of step then being developed by Johansson, Bournonville's pupil, who had come to St Petersburg to take over that side of the training at the Imperial Academy. The few solos that Petipa allowed in his ballets to the male members of the cast were there only because the Tsar and the Director insisted. These were usually arranged by Ivanov, Petipa's assistant, or by the dancers themselves.

It is now known that Cecchetti arranged his own Blue Bird solo for the first performance of *The Sleeping Beauty* in which he also played Carabosse. Paul Gerdt, who danced the Prince and was the Tsar's own soloist, also arranged his own dance. But neither man danced *sur les pointes*.

Before Ashton created Bottom's dance in *The Dream*, only Nijinska used *pointes* for a male dancer. She used them first for Le Beau Gosse in *Le Train bleu*, and later to characterise a precious young Fop busily picking his way through her interpretation of Molière's *Les Fâcheux*, both roles brilliantly danced by Anton Dolin.

No! The *pointes* are not the finishing touch to the male dance. It is enough for the man to display the finish of each step in Petipa's vocabulary by following the choreographer's flow of line, no matter in which style or for which choreographer.

Index

Bold numbers refer to illustrations.